ROMANCE WITH VOLUPTUOUSNESS

Expanding Frontiers:
Interdisciplinary Approaches to
Studies of Women, Gender, and Sexuality

SERIES EDITORS:
Karen J. Leong
Andrea Smith

ROMANCE WITH
VOLUPTUOUSNESS

Caribbean Women and Thick Bodies in the United States

KAMILLE GENTLES-PEART

University of Nebraska Press | Lincoln and London

Library of Congress Cataloging-in-Publication Data
Names: Gentles-Peart, Kamille, author.
Title: Romance with voluptuousness: Caribbean
women and thick bodies in the United States /
Kamille Gentles-Peart.
Description: Lincoln: University of Nebraska Press, [2016] |
Series: Expanding frontiers: interdisciplinary approaches
to studies of women, gender, and sexuality |
Includes bibliographical references and index.
Identifiers: LCCN 2016007771
ISBN 9780803290808 (cloth: alk. paper)
ISBN 9780803295131 (epub)
ISBN 9780803295148 (mobi)
ISBN 9780803295155 (pdf)
Subjects: LCSH: Women, Black—Caribbean Area. |
Immigrant women—United States. | Caribbean Americans—
Cultural assimilation. | Body image—United States. | Femi-
nine beauty (Aesthetics)—United States. | Feminine beauty
(Aesthetics)—Caribbean Area. | Racism—United States.
Classification: LCC HQ1501 .G467 2016 |
DDC 305.4896/9729—dc23
LC record available at http://lccn.loc.gov/2016007771

Designed and set in Arno Pro by L. Auten.

For Elizabeth, my darling daughter

CONTENTS

ACKNOWLEDGMENTS

It really takes a community to undertake and complete a project such as this, a team of people who directly and indirectly make it possible to research and think and write and persevere. I had such people throughout the duration of this project, and they deserve to be recognized. I am in debt to the women who trusted me with their stories, who invited me into their living rooms, kitchens, workplaces, and social groups, and who liberally shared their (sometimes agonizing) thoughts about their bodies. I am grateful to Roger Williams University and the Foundation for the Promotion of Teaching and Scholarship, which provided the institutional and financial support for the research and writing of the manuscript. My editor from the University of Nebraska Press, Alicia Christensen; series editors Andrea Smith and Karen Leong; and the anonymous reviewers of the manuscript were also invaluable in the process—their critique and encouragement helped to mold the project and text into their current form. I am also thankful to Afshan Jafar and Erynn de Casanova, who helped to refine early versions of the work that inspired this larger project. I would also like to thank my colleagues and friends who read, commented, critiqued, and encouraged: Julia Jordan-Zachery, Keisha-Khan Perry, Anjali Ram, Hume Johnson, and Karen Flynn.

My personal support system shouldered much of the burden of this project and needs to be celebrated. I am grateful for my parents, Errol and Audrey

Gentles, whose sacrifice and continued support propel me to go further, and my sister, Keresha Gentles-Jones, who inspires me to be bold. I am also thankful for my grandmother Mary Adassa Littlejohn-McEwan (1922–2015), who did not live to see this manuscript completed, but who always supported and loved. I am blessed to have my friends Kadine Wallace, Sydonie Hickling, Bridget Saulsbury, and Shermel Millard, who listen, pray, and encourage. Finally, I am grateful to Samantha Peart and Royesha Johnson, who helped with the task of transcribing the hours of interviews and focus group sessions.

None of this would have been possible without the patience and love of Prince Peart; thank you, my love, for allowing me to pursue my dreams, for entertaining our little one in hotel rooms while I "did my thing," for making it possible to have my family share my professional space, for helping to keep me focused and grounded, for being a rock. I am grateful for Elizabeth Peart, my Lizzie-Bear, who makes me want to make the world a safe place for her to be a black girl.

Finally, I am grateful to the Promise-Keeper, in whom I live and move and have my being.

Earlier versions of portions of chapter 2 have appeared in "Adapting America: West Indian Women's Cultural Adaption of the American Diasporic Space," in *The Theme of Cultural Adaptation in American History, Literature, and Film: Cases When the Discourse Changed*, ed. Lawrence Raw, Tanfer Tunc, and Gulriz Buken (Edwin Mellen Press, 2009), 297–313; "'I'm Not American; Don't Forget It': West Indian Women, Difference and Cultural Citizenship in the United States," *Wadabagei: A Journal of the Caribbean and Its Diasporas* 15, nos. 1–2 (2014).

Earlier versions of portions of chapters 2, 3, and 4 have appeared in "West Indian Women, Body Politics and Cultural Citizenship," in *Bodies without Borders*, ed. Afshan Jafar and Erynn de Casanova (Palgrave MacMillan Press, 2013), 25–44.

Earlier versions of portions of chapter 5 have appeared in "'Fiwi TV': Ethnic Media and the West Indian Diaspora," *International Journal of Cultural Studies* 17, no. 6 (2014).

ROMANCE WITH VOLUPTUOUSNESS

1 THE "THICK BLACK WOMAN"
Racialized Body Politics and the Marginalization of Black Women

Reflections of a *Mahgah* Jamaican Woman

I always ate at least three meals a day. Being a graduate student with little disposable income, these meals were neither remarkable nor sophisticated; my daily diet usually consisted of oatmeal for breakfast, cheap fast food for lunch, and chicken with rice for dinner. Regardless of the simplicity and lack of variety of these dishes, I did not want to miss meals, because that would risk me hearing the dreaded words from my mother when I returned home between semesters: "You lose weight!" Many women would welcome these words and deem them a positive assessment of their bodies. However, as a woman from Jamaica, those words were distressing. It was important for me to "keep on some weight"; I did not want to be skinny. I had to "have shape"; I had to have thick hips and round buttocks.[1] So I was careful to eat.

This relationship with my body did not begin with graduate school in the United States; I was always petite and always desired to be as big and voluptuous—and thus as attractive—as my relatives and peers. I was also accustomed to having the deviance of my body being the topic of conversation at family gatherings and being highlighted by members of my community, particularly, but not limited to, females. Aunts, cousins, and girlfriends surveiled my body, liberally and jovially making comments about its small size and shape. Commentary also came indirectly from Jamaican popular culture with songs, magazines, and music videos promoting a body type that was not mine and reinforcing the difference of my body.

Emigration to the United States did little to change the expectation that my body conform to the Jamaican ideal. I was surrounded by mainstream American media prolific with thin images, but in the black Caribbean community of New York City where I resided and among my black Caribbean relatives and peers, a thick body was desirable. On the other hand, however, my body was perceived with admiration among my white American peers in the small midwestern town in the United States where I attended graduate school. My race and foreign accent marked me as "other" in this predominantly white space, but my small body size, which approximated the thin ideal of mainstream America, engendered some acceptance; it was one of the few areas of my person that I knew fit into the dominant discourses of my new home. My thin body did not fit the body type associated with blackness, and to some (both black and white Americans) that made me not "black" enough, and lacking in the erotic sexuality ascribed to black women. However, to many, I became exceptional; my small, "not black enough" body, in combination with my accent, made me foreign, other, exotic.

I am cognizant that being called "exotic" is problematic, as it marked me as different, not normal, a bit of a spectacle. However, this exoticization gave me increased access to mainstream American society. It created the perception that I was less aggressive, less confrontational, less threatening, all issues that I witness many bigger women in my community contending with when engaging with white American spaces, such as academia. In my experience, black women with bigger bodies are not only hypervisible in academia, but they are also marginalized. In fact, they often exist along the Mammy-Sapphire continuum (Henderson, Hunter, and Hildreth 2010). I believe that both ideologies of Mammy and Sapphire construct black femininity in ways that link thick black female bodies to ideas of lowered intelligence: Mammy is the big black domestic worker, Sapphire is her voluptuous, more feisty counterpart, and neither of them is very bright. Perceived along this continuum, black women in academia (and I would argue particularly those with bigger bodies that most align with these popular cultural images of black women) are systemically shut out of the intellectual life of the white-dominated academy of the United States. They routinely receive negative student and peer evaluations that describe them as militant and aggressive, they are often denied tenure as their work and contributions are viewed as less valuable and less deserving of compensation and promotion, their expertise and knowledge are often questioned and challenged (Jones and Shorter-Gooden 2004), and they are perceived and treated as the "maids of academe" (Harley 2008), supportive agents whose primary reason for existing is to help others (Bova 2000). I believe my smaller body helped to neutralize and "soften" the threat that Eurocentric imperialism has ascribed to thick black female bodies.

My thin, petite frame was also better for learning European dance forms such as ballet and modern dance, and I gravitated toward these performance arts. Admittedly, my body was not the ideal type for these dance forms, but they provided a space where the smallness of my thighs, hips, and buttocks were at least accepted (unlike in the mainstream Jamaican dance context, where big buttocks and thighs are prerequisites). Over time, I also noticed that my bigger-bodied relatives and friends in the diaspora no longer completely ridiculed my size; they viewed my body with a sense of ambivalence, of amusement but also admiration. They too noticed the mobility and inclusion (albeit marginal) that my body afforded me in the U.S. environment. They did not want my body, but they realized that it gave me access to American society in a way that theirs did not.

I continued to monitor my weight for years to come, nurturing my petite frame but making sure that I maintained my "shape." I appreciated and wanted to preserve the space created by my body in white mainstream society, but I also wanted a body that was acceptable to my black Caribbean counterparts. This negotiation also extended to my self-presentation, how I groomed and dressed my hybrid body. Growing up in Jamaica, in addition to having the voluptuous body, women were also expected to be of good character, meaning maintaining and projecting controlled sexuality and respectability, always being vigilant of the reputation being cultivated. Of course, this expectation of sexual purity for black Caribbean women contradicts the desire for and highly sensual position of the buttock in black Caribbean body politics (Wilk 1993), but as in many other cultures, women were expected to embody these traits simultaneously. Dress (the style, fit, and appropriateness of clothing and hair) was used as a major signifier of this propriety; women's presentation of self in public spaces was indicative of their social position and worth and was particularly significant in black Caribbean women's body politics.

From a very young age, I understood this politics of respectability. There were unwritten guidelines that prescribed the type of attire to be worn to particular places or on given occasions, as well as the condition that these clothes should be in. For example, I recall there being a clear distinction between clothing worn in public and those donned in the home. In addition to sleepwear, there was a set of comfortable "house" clothes that I wore within the confines of my home and the surrounding yard, and that were never worn beyond the domestic space. I was not allowed to wear these garments "on the road" as they were considered unsuitable for participation in public life. My "good" clothes (usually the newest, most fashionable, or least damaged) were reserved for appearances in public. These garments should be in great condition, with no visible stains, rips, or wrinkles. In fact, clothes donned in public should be well ironed and starched when necessary.

Public attire was also distinguished by occasion. While it was perfectly acceptable for me to wear jeans to markets, fetes, barbeques, and other outdoor outings, they were certainly inappropriate for "special" functions, which in Jamaican culture included balls, award programs, graduations, weddings, and receptions. Additionally, given the prominence of religion in Jamaica, and the high level of socialization that occurs within and around churches, attire for church services and functions was the most formal and exclusive. My "Sunday best" (usually a formal skirt suit or dress with matching shoes and other accessories) could only be worn to church or on very special occasions. Failure to wear clothing that met these standards was a direct indication of poor living conditions, poverty, low class, and lack of propriety. Violating these guidelines reflected negatively on one's class status, especially for women, creating a reputation that had long-lasting and detrimental effects in a society that valued respectability as a significant part of femininity.

My socialization related to dress and grooming did not always translate well into the American culture. While the African American communities I engaged with display similar principles about self-presentation, offering some refuge, the predominantly white spaces that I occupied valued a very different aesthetic. Even after living in the United States for several years, I still do not fully comprehend rules around dress that govern white American communities, particularly for semiformal, formal, and professional contexts. I have been embarrassed more times than I care to remember by being overdressed for events such as weddings, graduations, and award ceremonies that my cultural sensibilities deemed formal. I still recall the thinly veiled patronizing looks and comments I received that expressed a mixture of amusement, pity, and condescension at my over-dressed body. On those occasions, the liminality of my body was placed in sharp relief: my small frame engendered admiration, but groomed in the wrong way, it signaled unsophistication and became a *pappy-show* (a site of spectacle). On the other hand, as I began to make adjustments to my dress code in response to my current American contexts, I found myself often underdressed for Jamaican formal events and feeling out of touch with the Jamaican community. Now, for every event, I am careful to take note of whether it is a Jamaican or (white) American setting, to inquire about the host of the event and who will be in attendance, and adjust my outfits accordingly; in other words, I have learned to regulate my dress and self-presentation based on the cultural context within which the function is located.

I continue to stand out as one of the few persons who "dress up" for my job as a professor. Students, faculty, and staff frequently comment on my style, but also on the level of smartness that characterizes my everyday office wear. Of course, interpreted within the context of the Jamaican culture, my dress is relatively moderate and even borders on conservative, but when viewed through the prism of white (predominantly middle-class) sensibilities, I am an outlier. I am fully aware that my choice to at least partially perpetuate the Jamaican standards for self-grooming exacerbates my simultaneous hypervisibility and erasure in my majority white institution, giving fuel to existing discourses that foreground my body but ignore my intellect. However, this problematic and complex visibility fostered by the intersection of race, class, gender, body size, and dress is preferable again to the invisibility that plagues many black women who are located in academic institutions shaped by Eurocentrism and imperialism. Therefore, similar to my negotiation of body size and shape, I am ever conscious of my grooming, wanting to foster a type of self-presentation that affords access (though problematic in some instances) into Jamaican and dominant American social and cultural spaces.

In this way, my body is a major site for my negotiation of belonging and subjectivity in the United States. My body size and dress are corporeal manifestations of my multiple and simultaneous registers of otherness and belonging as a black Caribbean woman living in the United States; indeed, my shape, size (as well as my hair and complexion), the general presentation of my body, and my careful management of them are reflections of my diasporic identity and my struggle for inclusion in the multiple and sometimes conflicting spaces I traverse.

My experience is not simply anecdotal; it is a common narrative within the black Caribbean diaspora. Surveillance and regulation of women's bodies (though based on a bigger body type) occur in the English-speaking Caribbean as in the global North. Unlike some popular and scholarly belief, however, this surveillance to maintain a bigger ideal is neither healthy nor innocuous. Rather, these processes have fostered disordered eating habits such as an obsession with eating, as seen in my case, as well as the consumption of copious amounts of weight-enhancing dietary supplements, such as ingesting "fowl pills," hormones given to chickens to make them plump.

Women from the English-speaking Caribbean thus come to the United States already habituated to pursuing an ideal beauty. However, migration requires these women to engage not only with beauty discourses cultivated in the Caribbean but also with those fostered outside their cultural homes and norms, specifically the Western beauty ideals of the United States. Furthermore, both sets of beauty regimes are tied to ideologies of value and personal worth and are used to create and police boundaries of dominant spaces. Black Caribbean women entering the United States therefore are not only negotiating issues of body image engendered by Caribbean and American pressures to maintain a certain body; they are also contending with discourses and practices around the body that aim to marginalize and exclude them from economic, social, and political spaces in the United States. *Romance with Voluptuousness* is an examination of the negotiation of these processes. At the heart of this book is an attempt to understand the ways in which beauty regimes are exercised, experienced, and resisted through the body of immigrant black women in the United States.

Romance with Voluptuousness sets out to map black Caribbean women's differentiated experiences with their voluptuous beauty ideal in the United States. The term "romance" draws on Belinda Edmondson's definition of the concept as the idealization of ideas and archetypes, in this case those that have come to represent Caribbean society and Caribbeanness in European American and intra-Caribbean discourses (1999, 2). As Edmondson explains, "'Romance' of particular tropes and paradigms identified with an essential Caribbeanness (such as carnival and cultural hybridity, to name two of the more striking examples) marks the process by which concrete ideological-political issues are mystified into regional symbols divorced from their ideological context" (2).

One such ideological trope is that of the voluptuous black woman. Using the actual reports of women, *Romance with Voluptuousness* explores the "romance" that black Caribbean women in the United States have with this idealized beauty standard of the Caribbean and how they embody it in their own lives. Furthermore, this work examines the women's experiences with upholding these constructs in the United States and the cognitive and performative strategies they use to negotiate hegemonies of beauty and their real-life implications. This book is not a historical analysis of voluptuousness, nor does it offer an explanation of the place of the curvy figure in contemporary Caribbean body image. Rather, using the personal accounts of real women, the text explores how black women with heritage in the English-speaking Caribbean participate in, perpetuate, and struggle with this beauty standard of the black Caribbean while living in the United States. It foregrounds the complicated ways in which these immigrant women negotiate beauty standards in the diaspora and offers a different vantage point from which to view their migration experiences.

The "Thick Black Woman" as Controlling Image

During the colonial period (between the sixteenth and eighteenth centuries), European travelers writing about Africa drew on and contributed to a European discourse on black womanhood that ascribed a big body to all black women and used it as a signifier of otherness and lesser culture and intelligence. The depiction of colonized black women in these writings presented them as having monstrous (big), unwomanly bodies that were dangerously, aberrantly hypersexual, and not intended to be beautiful and admired (as the delicate bodies of their white counterparts).

Perhaps the most iconic figure in this regard is that of Saartjie Baartman, the so-called Hottentot Venus. Baartman, a South African slave, was brought to Europe in 1810 for the purposes of "displaying her enlarged genitals and buttocks" (Mason 2013, 687). Her body was exhibited across Europe as the epitome of African and black female sexual abnormality. As Simone Alexander (2014) states, in Western eyes, Baartman's deviant body shape and race fueled ideas of her "presumed hypersexuality" and subhuman qualities, and served as the basis for her exploitation and denial of citizenship; as "a member of the Khoisan herder tribe, Baartman, as a result of her endowed figure—her fleshy buttocks—her 'excess flesh,' became the object of desire and derision, fear and adoration. Baartman's inability to attain citizenship was a foregone conclusion, since her body, in many ways did not correspond to the national (read white) body" (24).

These traits—big buttocks, deviant sexuality, bestiality—were not only limited to Baartman; these ideologies about large posteriors intersecting with the notion of racialized inhumanity have been extended to *all* women of African descent. As Janell Hobson says, the long-lasting effect of these exhibitions of black women's bodies in European and American culture is that "black women *en masse* are often 'known' to have big behinds, à la the Hottentot Venus" (2003, 93, emphasis in original). Hobson continues: "Baartman . . . came to signify the 'ugliness' of her *race*. It is this connection between blackness and grotesquerie that has haunted many people of African descent, especially those living under the influence of dominant white culture, to the point that a slogan such as 'Black is beautiful' seems a radical statement" (94, emphasis in original).

These "monstrous," dangerous bodies were also used to signify and justify black women's only utility as producers of crops, bearers of children, and thus their dispensability in modern, capitalist society. This construction of the black female body as one built for functionality, for labor, was employed to affirm Europe's use of black slave labor (J. Morgan 1997, 168). In addition to the construction of black women as dangerous, the "Hottentot Venus" image also gave primacy to black women's "muscular capabilities, physical strength, aggressive carriage and sturdiness" and presented them as "devoid of feminine tenderness and graciousness" (Beckles 1999, 10). In other words, the image simultaneously perpetuated the masculinization of black women.[2] The "thick black woman" is therefore excluded from discourses of feminine beauty in the West.

The prevalence of the "thick black woman" ideology in contemporary white society—the idea that all black women are voluptuous (and thus not up to the standard of white beauty)—is a way to preserve the beauty ideology of the West as the domain of white women without overtly using racial discourses. According to Eduardo Bonilla-Silva (2006), in contemporary U.S. society, where the logic of color blindness reigns, racial inequality is perpetuated through strategies that mask racism by highlighting instead cultural and individual difference. This "new racism" functions to maintain the contemporary racial structure through subtle, institutional practices and helps to underscore white privilege without incriminating whites (Bonilla-Silva 2006). The idea of the "thick black woman" in mainstream American beauty discourses plays into this color-blind racism; by accepting and propagating the idea that black women are voluptuous and not thin, dominant American society can exclude black women from accepted categories of beauty without using race per se. Their bodies can be dismissed under the guise of cultural standards of beauty that do not align with those in the mainstream of the United States. In this sense, black women, including those of the Caribbean, can be marginalized as different without overtly using race; while race is central to black women's exclusion from beauty categories, the emphasis on their deviant bodies allows dominant society to explain their marginalization in nonracial terms.

Additionally, the idea that black women cannot and do not need to fit into dominant U.S. standards of beauty further dehumanizes them by recuperating a form of the "strong black woman" rhetoric. In her contemporary form, the "strong black woman" is "a motivated, hardworking breadwinner" who is "smart and sacrificial" with a "seemingly irrepressible spirit unbroken by a legacy of oppression, poverty, and rejection. . . . [She has the] ability to simply shake off or get past the formidable obstacles that face [her]" (Harris-Lacewell 2001, 3, 6). This superwoman is prolific in the white American imagination, fueled by the real experiences of black women, who seem to miraculously maintain their households in spite of poverty, and is prominent in African American popular culture. Through the media, the symbol of the "strong black woman" has been rehearsed and venerated to the detriment of real women, who are expected to emulate these ideological foils (Harris-Lacewell 2001). Through this "strong black woman" trope, black women are reified as indomitable and undaunted by oppressive systems but simultaneously indelicate, unfeminine, and ultimately "other" (Harris-Lacewell 2001; Beauboeuf-Lafontant 2009; Lau 2011).

The perception that black women fall outside the boundaries of thin aesthetics reflects this ideology. First, the bigger body that it prescribes for black women marks them as less delicate, less fragile, less dainty, and therefore more masculine; in other words, their bigger bodies make them less "woman" than white women. Second, the implication that black women do not have the body anxieties of their white counterparts draws on the notion that they can overcome issues that "normal" women face in their everyday lives, which again reinforces their fortitude, indelicateness, and unwomanliness.

African diaspora cultures, including those of the Caribbean, have since attempted to reclaim the "thick black woman" from her place of shame and humiliation, from her position as the negative counterpoint to white feminine beauty; they have, using Eve Sedgwick's phrase, "renegotiat[ed] . . . the representational contract" between the voluptuous black female body and the world (1990, 230). These cultures have radically ascribed value to the ample black female physique and have associated the slender body with the violence of colonization, desexualization, and economic dearth (Shaw 2006). This rewriting of the voluptuous black female body is epitomized, for example, by Grace Nichols's *The Fat Black Woman's Poems*, in which she fiercely interrogates and corrects the devaluation of blackness and the marginalization of the fat female subject. In poems such as "Beauty," which repeatedly declares that "beauty is a fat black woman" (1984, 7), and "Looking at Miss World," which challenges the primacy and celebration of the white European beauty ideals in this ironically named "world" pageant, Nichols convincingly makes the case for liberating black women from the Western standard of whiteness and thinness and reinstating them as worthy citizens.

In her reading of the poems, Alexander concludes that: "Fat Black Woman deconstructs the nation-state's definition of ideal citizenship, cross-examining the politics of identity and belonging and collapsing enforced boundaries and borders. . . . 'Performing her excess flesh' by choice, in contradistinction to Baartman, the Fat Black Woman presents a formidable challenge to black women's denial of citizenship and their assumed hypervisibility and hypersexuality" (2014, 130). While Nichols celebrates fatness and not just a curvy, voluptuous body, her work reflects the contemporary celebratory politics that surrounds black women who do not fit into the norms of slenderness upheld by Western societies.

As an inversion and rejection of the colonization project, anticolonialist discourse from the English-speaking Caribbean has also taken up the celebration of the voluptuous black woman. Colonialism entailed not only control of the land but also subjugation of the population by imposing Eurocentric ontological orientations unto them (Meeks 2000). Many postindependence movements in the so-called British West Indies and the larger Caribbean embody the rejection of this colonial ontology, reframing Africa as the motherland and cultivating notions of black empowerment (Bogues 2002). As Deborah Thomas (2004) notes, there emerged a representation of "modern blackness" in the Caribbean that engaged and rejected the Western vision of progress and development.

This reimagining also included celebration of the black female body. In her analysis of beauty contests in early postcolonial Jamaica, Rochelle Rowe (2009) highlights the ways in which black women's bodies were used to construct a new national identity apart from its colonialist history. She notes that, in a time when white and brown elites made attempts to construct and project a racially harmonious New World identity, African Jamaican elites, reflecting African diaspora thought, challenged the low position of the black woman by elevating her in society through the Miss Ebony contest. In contrast to the existing Miss Jamaica contest, which crowned only women of white or light brown skin tones, the Miss Ebony contest celebrated dark-skinned black women, raising the possibility of a desirable and respectable black femininity in a time when they were marginalized (Rowe 2009). Granted, this contest was meant to create an "iconic imagery of black femininity" that was modern and sophisticated (Rowe 2009, 49), which meant that she was slim, but for the first time in the region, the black female body was recast in a positive light.

The voluptuous black female body has also been recast in a more positive light. Perhaps the most famous instance of the reframing of the voluptuous black Caribbean woman is the legend of Nanny of the Maroons in Jamaica. Nanny, a fugitive slave in the eighteenth century, is credited with forming the Maroon community in the hills of Jamaica, and with famously defeating English armies by catching bullets with her buttocks and hurling them back at her attackers (Sharpe 2002). Here, the voluptuous black female body is presented and reified as essential to the emancipatory movements of Jamaica and the fight against bondage and imperialism.

The voluptuous female body has also been embraced by the majority of the poor and working-class black people in the English-speaking Caribbean, a move that asserts distance from and nonconformity to the European upper-class moral ideals that operated among black Caribbean elites. Similar to what occurred in nineteenth-century Europe and perpetuating ideas from the colonial period, brown or non-black Caribbean elites created a moral typography in which working-class black women were deemed vulgar, uncontrollable, and dangerous, and their bodies (conceived as always already voluptuous in shape) became markers of their excessive sexuality and lack of restraint. As Bibi Bakare-Yusuf says about this phenomenon, "the voluptuous black female body came to embody upper-class anxiety over the moral status of the lower class" (2006, 467). In embracing the ample, black female body, women excluded from the elite class (the vast majority of black women in the English-speaking Caribbean) rejected the negativity associated with voluptuousness, and celebrated "an unruly voluptuosity—the joy of being fat" (Bakare-Yusuf 2006, 470).

Of course, not all black female bodies are accepted within the black Caribbean, nor are all voluptuous bodies celebrated. Indeed, it is important to note that there is a difference between a voluptuous body and fatness in the celebratory politics of black women. In most instances, the positive discourses about black womanhood are in relation to the former, a black body with ample derrière, hips, and thighs, not one that is round and plump. Therefore, within this construction of black femininity, fat black women continue to be marginalized. The presence of their bodies allows other black women to "assume the posture of their white counterparts by recognizing themselves to varying degrees as being physiologically what the fat black woman is not" (Shaw 2005, 151). Furthermore, black women of low socioeconomic status with fat or thick bodies—such as the higglers in Kingston, Jamaica (Winnifred Brown-Glaude 2011) or the dance-hall queens—continue to be viewed negatively in Caribbean societies. Their bodies epitomize unfeminine, out-of-order behavior, and rather than being celebrated, they are economically and socially marginalized.

Furthermore, color (not necessarily race) is also important. While one can argue that conceptions of beauty in the wider U.S. society operate on a black/white dichotomy, conceptions of beauty within Caribbean and African American communities operate through colorism, a color continuum that privileges light skin. Colorism is related to skin color but differs from racism in that the latter discriminates based on racial categorization while the former discriminates based on complexion. This system of colorism dates back to the slavery and colonialism eras in the Caribbean and Americas, when lighter skin color (a heuristic of closeness to whiteness) was used as a pervasive marker of social power. Therefore, "mulattos," the brown-skinned offspring of the white masters and black slave women, gained prestige under this system on the basis of their lighter complexion (Charles 2010). This color hierarchy is perpetuated in contemporary black communities, where people (particularly women) of light brown complexion are given economic, social, and political privilege. Brown people in these communities represent "a class of people, the post-colonial inheritors of privilege and status passed on by the white upper class" (Mohammed 2000, 35). It is no wonder, then, that the practice of "bleaching" has become commonplace in black communities; people use various techniques to lighten their skin color, not because they want to be white but because they want to be brown or light skinned and gain access to the social and cultural capital that comes with light-skin privilege.

Colorism also figures largely in the construction of black female beauty ideologies. As Patricia Mohammed (2000) shows, in slave society in the Caribbean, "mulatto" women (light-skinned women with African physicality [Hope 2011]) emerged as desirable objects of beauty and became the subjects of poems and songs during this time. Painters such as Agostino Brunias (*The Barbados Mulatto Girl 1780*), authors, and travel writers made "mulatto" women the subject of their works, indicating the perceived beauty of women with a light complexion. Furthermore, even as images and discourses of black women with thick bodies circulated in the colonial and independence eras of the Caribbean (that both denigrate and celebrate black womanhood), these were juxtaposed against images of brown ("mulatto") women, who were upheld as ideal femininity and beauty (Charles 2011; Hope 2011). Featuring subjects who often had thin bodies as well as light skin, the images of these women contrasted not only the complexion of the "thick black woman" but also the body type; while the darker-skinned woman was thick (and grotesque and manly), the lighter-skinned woman was thin (and beautiful and more feminine).

The prominence of the brown-skinned woman is still apparent in contemporary Caribbean societies, as evidenced in the higher social positions of light-skinned women as well as the continued practice of crowning light-skinned straight-haired ("pretty hair") women as beauty queens (Barnes 2000). In this way, then, I argue that Mohammed's (2000) analysis of Jamaican society (through her reflections on singer Buju Banton's songs "Love Mi Browning" and "Love Black Woman") rings true: there may be a respect for black women (on the basis of political awareness and national and racial identification), but that does not necessarily translate into desire or attraction. In postcolonial Caribbean societies, the "thick black woman" is revered and even reified as a part of antislavery, anticolonial discourse, but in real life, it is the "browning" or "red woman" who is considered desirable and womanly. (Of course, neither of these positions is desirable as in both cases, black and brown women are dehumanized and mobilized for the agendas of masculine ethos [Mohammed 2001; Hope 2011].) Clearly, ideal feminine beauty in the Caribbean is tied to colorism and is undergirded by the "discursive process via which the brown or mulatto class gained hegemonic ascendancy in Jamaica" (Hope 2011, 167). Color matters in the discourse of black female beauty, and while colorism is not the focus of this text, it is a significant part of any discussion of beauty and social hierarchy, in both the islands and the United States.

That said, the voluptuous black female body (the "thick black woman" image), while not the most valued within elite circles, is embedded in Afro-Caribbean history, culture, and identity and is tied to ideas of nationhood, independence, and anticolonialism. Black Caribbean postcolonial politics celebrate the fleshy black female body, undermining the slender Eurocentric ideal and its accompanying codes of femininity, respectability, and civility. However, as Natasha Barnes (2000) cautions, the constitution of black women as desirable feminine subjects within Western frameworks has uneven emancipatory potential. Speaking of the many titles and identities given to and claimed by black women, Hortense Spillers also observes that "they are markers so loaded with mythical prepossession that there is no easy way for the agents buried beneath them to come clean" (1987, 65). Similarly, Samantha Murray, in her engagement with fat acceptance movements in the United States that encourage fat women to change their attitudes toward their bodies, has realized that it is no simple task to remove women from discourses that constitute them as subjects, from the "ingrained body knowledges about the offensiveness of the [deviant] female body" (2005, 159). In other words, efforts to reframe deviant bodies in new, enabling, and politically empowering ways are not automatically transformative and unambiguous.

So renegotiating the "contract" between the image of black femininity (that is, the always already voluptuous black woman) and the world in which it is situated does not completely decouple it from its history in modern imperialistic designs and its dominant ideologies nor from the "knowledges" that have become so embedded in society. People of the English-speaking Caribbean and the wider African diaspora cannot fully eschew European beauty sensibilities by simply inverting them, as they are a part of their histories; the inversion and co-optation of the "thick black woman" do not erase or replace the colonialist and racist ideologies associated with the voluptuous black female body. In spite of being reclaimed and inverted, the "thick black woman" ideology remains a tool used by colonizers to undergird ideas about black women's role and worth in modern society as reproducers and laborers. These ideologies about race, body size, and social worth that are embedded in the image continue to be perpetuated and underscored in Eurocentric societies as well as among *black* people aspiring toward white European ideals. In the current Eurocentric global hegemony, thick bodies are used to signal the "pathology" of black femaleness and their subsequent worthlessness; they preserve the idea that the bodies of black women, particularly those from the global South, are monstrous, rape-able, disposable, and useful only for reproduction and field (blue-collar) labor.

The figure of the "thick black woman" thus has an ambiguous place in Caribbean societies and the African diaspora; it is used to celebrate the curvy black female body (thus providing a counternarrative to hegemonic conceptions of beauty that associates beauty with whiteness and thinness), but it may also contribute to the marginalization of real black women. This is not to say that we should put an end to black women celebrating thick bodies, but it is worth recognizing and interrogating the ways in which the acceptance of the "thick black woman" ideology, the construction of this single body type for black women, was (and still is) used to characterize all black women and justify their devaluation in modern spaces. As Murray asks, how effective is the simple reversal from a negative body to a celebrated one when "the system of judgment that positions the [big black] body as a negative body remains intact" (2005, 162)?

For this reason, we need to "map out the complicated meanings and mixed benefits of black women's age-old desire to be fully constituted as 'women' in a Western conceptual categorization that has traditionally made women of colour its 'Other'" (Barnes 2000, 105). While I fully agree with Hobson that "black women . . . must confront the prevailing imagery of grotesque derrières and black female hypersexuality to distinguish the myths and lies from our own truths and the ways in which we wish to represent ourselves" (2003, 103), I would add that we should also challenge the very *idea* of the "batty," the big derrière, in our conception of black womanhood. It is not enough to simply reverse perceptions of the voluptuous black female body; we have to critically engage with the regime that creates these ideas in the first place in order to dismantle it.

Answering the call by Edmondson (1999) to question Caribbean "romances," in this text I critically examine the normalization of the "thick black woman" as black Caribbean womanhood in the Caribbean diaspora in the United States. Like Edmondson I ask, "How do old romanticized images of the region [specifically the voluptuous black female body], initially constructed in the imperial European and American imagination, reinvent themselves in discourses that apparently come from the newly independent, decolonized Caribbean subjects themselves?" (1999, 6). Furthermore, I ask, to what extent does this beauty standard impact the women's psychic, social, and economic well-being in the United States, and how do they negotiate the challenges that arise because of their bodies?

There have been many studies about the black female body that explore the intersection of their race, gender, and body type in dominant Caribbean societies. For example, in her study of dance-hall culture in Jamaica, Carolyn Cooper (1995, 2004) reinterprets dance-hall culture and the bodies of voluptuous black women who are the subjects and audiences of dance-hall music. Throughout her work, she insists that we recognize the liberatory space that dance-hall culture creates for black women through its lyrics that celebrate their body type and its culture, allowing black women to invert roles and mores constructed by classist and racist European society. Bakare-Yusuf (2006) has also looked at the voluptuous women of the Jamaican dance hall and their self-expressions through dress. She argues that presenting their bodies as a site of spectacle, dance-hall women create a world and state of being that challenge Eurocentric and gendered ideas about femininity and womanhood. Barnes (2000) presents the ambiguous position of women's bodies in Trinidad's carnival. She demonstrates how their presence (bodies) in this very public and global event can signal women's empowerment even as it reenacts male patriarchal stereotypes of women as sexually available. Carole Boyce-Davies (2010) also explores the black Caribbean female body. She examines how these women claim space and empowerment in present-day carnival and dance-hall culture in the Caribbean.

I expand this discussion of black Caribbean women's bodies by focusing on how real women in the black Caribbean diaspora engage with the fetishized and controversial voluptuous black female body, and the way that race, gender, and nationality intersect with beauty standards to influence their lives in the United States. By using the reports of actual women as evidence, I contribute to the creation of a holistic picture of the construction of black Caribbean femininity. The experiences of actual women presented here provide a human, embodied, subjective element that complements existing analyses of cultural texts and forms. It gives voice to these women's own interpretations of and engagement with the black female body upheld in the Caribbean. In this sense, the text adds to literature about these women but also empowers them by foregrounding their experiences and taking their words seriously; the text centers the knowledges that these women make in their everyday lives.

Additionally, by focusing on black Caribbean women in the diaspora, this text allows us to see how black Caribbean embodied femininity is constructed and enacted outside the borders of Caribbean islands. This inquiry is particularly important given the significance of transnational migration in Caribbean societies, and the continuous and increasing interchange of cultural ideas between the Caribbean islands and their diasporas; what black Caribbean women are doing in New York City, for example, reverberates in and influences the lived experiences of women in the Caribbean and vise versa. So by studying diasporic Caribbean women's "romance" with voluptuousness, this text highlights the transnational flow of beauty ideals and explores ideas about beauty in the diaspora that reflect and shape those of the islands.

Negative Physical Capital and Black Diasporic Women

Given the links between the voluptuous ideal of the Caribbean and Eurocentric discourses, black Caribbean women in the United States who maintain "romances" with this ideal not only recuperate colonialist discourses but make themselves susceptible to discriminating economic and social practices of the global North. Of course there are other interlocking pragmatic factors that affect the lives of immigrant black women from the Caribbean. For instance, immigration status, education level, and age can all influence their social and economic mobility. However, embodied factors can and do exacerbate (or minimize) the issues they face by further policing their access to certain spaces. The use of race, gender, and nationality in exclusionary economic and social practices is well documented (Omi and Winant 2014; Bonilla-Silva 2006). I add that body size and shape are also important factors to consider when understanding the marginalization of immigrant black women in the United States.

The use of bodies and appearance to determine inner characteristics, morals, and mental abilities has a long history in the Western Hemisphere. In the eighteenth century, Johann Kaspar Lavater recuperated the deterministic link between beauty and morality in his science of physiognomy. He believed that the essence of man was his soul and that the body was a mirror into that soul. Physiognomy, the science (or art) of judging character from facial characteristics, was thus a tool to discover the true self, the inner being (Wegenstein 2012). In this way, Lavater propagated a physiognomic culture of seeing that trained the eye to see in certain ways and make judgments about people's abilities and worth based on the visible aspects of their bodies.

Furthermore, Lavater's theory of physiognomy laid the foundation for the naturalization of the link between morality and physical deviance, the belief that biology and physical makeup determine mental and moral character, and eugenics, "a sociopolitical program for creating a world that has rid itself of deviant groups" (Wegenstein 2012, 27). Each of these ideas was used to establish European men as superior and to marginalize and oppress women and non-European peoples, particularly Africans. For example, in the nineteenth century, Italian psychiatrist Cesare Lombroso popularized and normalized the biological determinism of criminals. He claimed that all criminals have similar facial traits, including low, sloping foreheads, overdeveloped cheekbones and jaws, dark skin, thick and curly hair, and long arms. Lombroso found these characteristics to be more prominent and prolific among the black and Mongol races, clearly establishing the relationship between black bodies and immoral character and reinforcing the dichotomy between good European white people and deviant, immoral people of other races. Similarly, Samuel R. Wells, a professor of phrenology, believed that the Caucasian race had superior skulls that made them superior humans. He said that the shape and form of the Caucasian skull indicates "great intellectual power, strong moral or spiritual sentiments, and a . . . moderate development" compared to other "less advanced races" (quoted in Wegenstein 2012, 31).

Variations of the physiognomic culture of seeing continue to persist today, particularly in relation to who is allowed access to economic, political, and social spheres. Now, as in the eighteenth century, bodies do have an impact on people's ability to attain social and economic power; the appearance of the body is used to determine people's suitability to participate in these spaces in the society. According to Pierre Bourdieu (1986), physicality (that is, the "size, shape and appearance of the flesh" [Shilling 2004, 474]) is symbolically valued in social fields (ideological spaces) and helps to determine the accumulation of other forms of capital or social power. The effective conversion of this physical capital into social power is contingent on the subject's ability to develop his or her body in ways that are recognized as possessing value in the social field; the more one's body mirrors or successfully replicates the dominant body ideals of the social space, the more one is valued and the more opportunities one has to convert this physical capital into social, cultural, and economic gain (Bourdieu 1986).

Furthermore, for Bourdieu there are clear class-based distinctions in how the body is perceived, treated, and presented in a social field. Specifically, in the global North, the working classes, with little leisure time to cultivate their bodies, are said to subsequently develop an instrumental, functional relationship to their bodies characterized by a "free and easy attitude" toward food and drink (Bourdieu 1984, 185). In contrast, the dominant, wealthier classes value bodies cultivated through reserve and control and are able to treat their bodies as projects and take a more organized approach to their consumption of food. These class-based significations of the body have great consequences for social mobility. As Chris Shilling says: "There are substantial inequalities in the symbolic values accorded to particular bodily forms. While typical working-class bodies are not without symbolic value . . . , their accent, posture, bearing and dress are generally not valued highly. In contrast, the dominant classes are more able to produce bodily forms of highest value as they possess the spare time and money necessary for their formation. Thus, different bodily forms are implicated in the production of unequal quantities and qualities of physical capital" (2004, 477).

In the global North, then, one's attainment of physical capital is hindered not only by the conditions of actual bodies but also by gendered, classist, and racist discourses that circulate in society about certain types of bodies. Within these societies, the white, male, slender (read reserved, regulated) body, usually associated with middle-class whiteness, is perceived as the most intellectually productive and desirable. On the other hand, bigger bodies, usually perceived as the "natural" state of the working-class and poor, are viewed as ideal for low-status jobs (laborers) and are associated with low mental capacity. In this way, then, body aesthetics are used to codify differences between those who are allowed social, economic, and political power in society and those who are not; they create a system of social and economic stratification in which people are automatically positioned at the top or bottom of the hierarchy based on ideologies about the size, shape, and appearance of the body. Those with bodies that do not align with the dominant ideals of the society face social and economic discrimination, or negative physical capital.

The impact of gendered, racialized, and classed body politics is very evident in the United States. In 2001 the United States declared a government-sanctioned "war against obesity," the latest manifestation of a historical trend to curb obesity in its citizens (Herndon 2005). However, as April Michelle Herndon (2005) convincingly shows, this "fatwa" against obesity (taken up by doctors, public health practitioners, and journalists) is ultimately a war against people who are fat: obesity, while acknowledged as being largely influenced by the proliferation of fast-food chains and widening economic inequalities, is seen as primarily a problem of will, a result of a lack of self-control, and justifies and normalizes weight-based discrimination against people who are deemed fat. Fat bodies in public spaces are read as lazy, gluttonous, unhygienic, and weak (Murray 2005), and people who are considered fat face discrimination and exclusion from the mainstream, including the job market, the fashion industry, and the health-care system. Poor black women (owing to their supposed bigger body ideal, lack of concern about weight, and absence of social pressure to be thin) as well as immigrants (with their "un-American" food and eating habits) are marked as most at risk and thus the most problematic; they are routinely excluded from spaces of economic and social power on this basis. Therefore, this "fatwa" targets and marginalizes those who are already disenfranchised in U.S. culture. Herndon makes the point that "as nightly news reports continue to suggest that the fattest people in the United States are people of color, immigrants, and members of the lower class, the war against obesity begins to target a specific group of people who are already, in some sense, second-class citizens" (2005, 128).

Evidently, in spite of fat-acceptance movements and the existence of black and brown communities that have bigger beauty standards for women, bigger bodies are marginalized in mainstream U.S. society. Black Caribbean women migrating to the United States enter a beauty hegemony that privileges and rewards the white and thin body while socially and economically marginalizing those who do not align with the accepted beauty ideals of mainstream America. Within this discourse, black women, particularly those who embody and pursue the "thick black woman" ideal, are in danger of being perceived as antithetical to the so-called restraint of the productive (valuable) classes of their new homes in the global North. They not only risk being deemed unattractive but face deeper marginalization in dominant American society. In this case, the negotiation of beauty ideologies for these women is not only a matter of cultivating self-esteem; such negotiations also have implications for procuring social and psychological well-being in a beauty hegemony that is hostile toward them. In this text, I examine the extent to which the combination of the gender, race, and body type of black Caribbean women in the United States may produce a form of negative physical capital that undermines and negates their accrual of social (and economic) empowerment.

Embodied Cultural Citizenship

The social field of the United States does not completely determine the embodied experiences of voluptuous black Caribbean women; these women wrestle with ideologies in their new home in an effort to resist marginalization and claim social and cultural agency. Women overall struggle with dominant beauty ideologies, but these confrontations are particularly salient for black Caribbean women relocating to Western countries. As postcolonial black women migrating to the global North, they must contend with power regimes of race, class, and gender but also struggle against and within Eurocentrism; they encounter ideologies that mark women from developing countries, such as those of the Caribbean, as backward and only good for service-oriented jobs.

Negotiating the multiplicative effect of their race, gender, body politics, and nationality is not a simple task. As Gayatri Spivak (1988) has demonstrated, because of discrepancies related to language and modes of representations, subaltern (or formerly colonized) cultures cannot be reconciled with the cultures of the West; the formers' experiences and realities are different from those of the ex-colonizers and are often framed in ways that reinforce their subjugation. In other words, for cultures that have been subordinated by colonialism, equitable dialogue with the colonizer is not possible. Therefore, the negotiations that black Caribbean women engage in with U.S. hegemonies (of race, gender, and body politics) are necessary and meaningful but never simple or completely transformative and liberatory.

Aihwa Ong (1996) contends that the complicated interactions between postcolonial, nonwhite immigrants and their new homes in the imperialistic global North foster cultural citizenship, the creation of personhood and visibility within societies that try to marginalize them. It involves the dual process of self-making (having control over one's person) as well as being-made (being acted upon by external forces) within "webs of power" that establish criteria of belonging (Ong 1996, 738). Similarly, Toby Miller (2006) sees cultural citizenship as the right to be known and speak in the cultural context of a dominant society. In other words, cultural citizenship refers to inclusion, recognition, and social justice created through the everyday cultural practices of marginalized and subordinated groups. In the context of immigrants, it is the creation of a livable life in the diaspora, a process of self-creation that struggles against but does not fully evade the hegemonic ideologies of their new countries of residence.

The body is also significant in theorizing and understanding this pursuit of cultural citizenship, as it is the basis on which postcolonial black immigrants are accepted or excluded in their new homes. Political, economic, and technological globalization has certainly changed the nature of international relations and migration, but it is the arrival and presence of actual bodies within national borders that challenge notions of nationhood. Specifically, the deterritorialization of nonwhite bodies from the global South has contested and complicated Western understandings of citizenship, identity, and cultural production and has triggered exclusionary practices toward these immigrants; bio-political factors such as race, ethnicity, gender, and religious and ethno-cultural manifestations (such as dress) influence nonwhite immigrants' entrance into geographic spaces. In other words, black immigrants from the global South encounter exclusion based on the visible aspects of their persons; their corporeality influences the extent to which they are ghettoized by society and the particular nature of their struggles for recognition.

Race and performances of religion and nation are important subjects that dominate much of the work on embodiment and embodied struggles in diasporas. However, the corporeal aspect of cultural citizenship is related not only to the ethnocultural and racial negotiation of black immigrants but also to negotiations of their body aesthetics, self-presentation, and self-fashioning. Immigrants' exclusion from citizenship in the global

North is often based on their race and nationality but also on their position outside Eurocentric beauty norms. Therefore, their negotiation of an acceptable life in their new homes necessarily entails negotiating spaces of self-esteem, positive body image, and corporeal value. Cultural citizenship (visibility and subjectivity) for postcolonial black immigrants is thus as much about negotiating with and within economic, political, state-based structures as it is about negotiating Eurocentric beauty regimes in the diasporic space.

I therefore contend that cultural citizenship for black Caribbean woman has body image dimensions that put their body aesthetic into sharp relief. Specifically, cultural citizenship for diasporic black women involves what I call *embodied cultural citizenship*, positive body image, self-concept, and physical capital amid the multiple beauty regimes and corresponding social obstacles they encounter in their new homes. It entails discursively constructing and presenting their bodies in ways that undermine and circumvent (though often reinscribe) the intersecting corporeal, social, and economic hegemonies of their diasporic space. (I use the term *embodied* to highlight the focus on negotiations that are centered around and manifested on the body and to distinguish it from other discussions that examine social and cultural, rather than physical and corporeal, productions of cultural citizenship.)

Shilling implicitly supports this notion of embodied cultural citizenship. Revising the causal relationship between body and social stratification presented by Bourdieu, he conceptualizes the body as "an unfinished biological and social phenomenon possessed of its own emergent properties . . . ; properties that can also be transformed, within certain limits, as a result of its entry into and participation in society" (2012, 15). Embodied subjects are thus understood as agents in society, possessing the ability to intervene and make a difference in their environment (Shilling 2005, 13). Bodies then are not passive; though they exist in broader structures of power that regulate them in various ways, they do have the capacity to reproduce, resist, and transform social meanings and norms.

Shilling later identifies three "modalities of action" that can be taken by embodied subjects in response to the social meanings ascribed to their bodies and the social relations they engender: "habitual" action refers to the reproduction of dominant norms within the social space; "embodied crisis" action refers to disruptions in the body's ability to imitate the social norms (such as when one's social field no longer values one's appearance) and is characterized by behavior oriented toward survival; "creative revelation" action refers to finding new ways to contend with the crises of physical capital and the obstacles created by having deviant bodies (2004, 481). This third modality of action can involve "the development of new skills, attitudes and behaviors that can lead to new opportunities for acquiring physical capital" (482).

Shilling's expansion of Bourdieu's theory of physical capital provides a starting point to help us articulate the embodied cultural citizenship of black Caribbean women in the United States. These women migrate to the global North and enter a social field in which the dominant white European beauty regime socially and economically marginalizes women of their race who hold their beauty ideologies; their raced, thick bodies are marked as unattractive and unvaluable in the society. This creates "embodied crisis" for these women, as the negative perception of their bodies have significant implications for their ability to fully participate in the social, economic, and political life of their new homes. Nevertheless, these black diasporic women have the ability to deviate from the trajectories assigned to them in the global North by their bodies; they can engage in "creative revelation" actions in which they construct discourses and behaviors that can lead to new opportunities for social and economic engagement and mobility in their new homes (Shilling 2004, 482).

Romance with Voluptuousness expands applications of Shilling's modalities of action. By addressing the body-society relationship of postcolonial diasporic women, I highlight the multiplicative effect of race, nationality, and body politics on women's "creative revelation" actions. As Winnifred Brown-Glaude states, "Bodies are multitextured. They are racialized, classed, gendered and sexualized (and so on) bodies, and so occupy multiple positions in any given time and space" (2011, 26). In order to assess the orientations and responses of embodied subjects, we thus have to highlight the multidimensional webs of power in which they are located, and not just one structural position. Black Caribbean women in the global North simultaneously straddle multiple social fields and ideological spaces, including those related to race, gender, and Eurocentrism. Additionally, they encounter various body politics. When they immigrate to Eurocentric locales, they do not discard their premigration beauty ideologies; they still engage with the beauty hegemonies of their homelands and also have to contend with the racialized, neocolonial body politics of their new homes in the global North. Therefore, they must negotiate ideologies informed by multiple discourses. This text recognizes the many discourses that surround black Caribbean immigrant women's bodies in the United States and explores the performative, cognitive, and material strategies they use to negotiate them.

Black Women and the Thin Ideal

Current research on and popular belief about body image hold that most black women in the United States are relatively unaffected by the dominant U.S. standards of thinness and develop a healthier body image than their white peers.[3] These ideas and research speak to the fact that black women in the United States have historically found ways to navigate the dominant ideas of beauty that are prevalent in mainstream, white society; they have found internal validation for their bodies in their intimate spheres as well as in their broader cultural communities (such as media targeting the black community.) Although I agree with these arguments, my goal is to offer a more nuanced and broader understanding of black women and body image. The text advocates for a more complex theorization of the relationship between black women and dominant white beauty ideals.

First, by explicating the ways in which black women of Caribbean heritage engage with the dominant beauty ideologies of the United States, the text foregrounds ethnicity; it adds questions about the influence of culture to the existing research on these processes. Furthermore, the text challenges the simple and limited ways in which black women's engagement with the white beauty ideal have been conceived, namely, the idea that they only reject it. Women of different racial, cultural, and ethnic heritage have the power to contest beauty ideals promoted within the dominant white society. This choice does not occur without struggle with the hegemonic ideals, however, and the resulting beauty discourses and performances are not always wholly empowering. Evidence of the negotiation of competing body discourses may be found among nonwhite women outside the United States. Research shows that these women develop a negotiated, rather than oppositional, body ideal and politics that comprise some resistive aspects but that also partially conform to the mainstream ideal. For example, Erynn de Casanova's study of Ecuadorian teenagers (2004) reveals that these young girls simultaneously hold white (Western) and Latin ideals. Casanova argues that her participants' inclusion of dress and personality in the definition of beauty mitigated the effect of the thin ideology disseminated by North American media, but their esteem of white prototypes simultaneously validated the thin, white ideal. Analogously, Fabienne Darling-Wolf (2004) has found that, even though the Japanese women in her study critiqued their local and Western media representations of beauty, these images informed their conception of attractiveness as young, thin, tall, light-skinned, and having bigger eyes.

In addition to adding considerations of ethnicity and dialogic negotiations to the literature on black women's engagement with the dominant standard of beauty in the United States, *Romance with Voluptuousness* also inserts explorations of the lived experiences of women who pursue a culturally sanctioned body aesthetic that is read negatively in white spaces. It examines the extent to which the race, nationality, and body type of black Caribbean women constrain their participation in U.S. society and affect their well-being.

Moreover, conspicuously absent from the literature is scholarship on the negotiations of diasporic women. While much has been written on how women engage with body politics that are imported into their cultural space, there is a dearth of literature on how women negotiate the hegemonic beauty discourses of the spaces they enter as immigrants. Even rarer are studies of how diasporic women contend with the dominant beauty regimes of their cultural heritage when they reside outside their homelands. *Romance with Voluptuousness* provides an intervention into the literature on body image by critically examining how black diasporic women work with and against beauty discourses of both the United States and the Caribbean.

The Caribbeanization of American Culture

There has been a black Caribbean presence in the United States since the slavery era (Chaney 1987). In fact, much of the slave population of the Carolinas and Louisiana came from the wholesale transfer of plantation owners and slaves from this region. Freed "West Indian" slaves were also present in New York City, and some were even active in the city during the American Revolutionary War (1775–83). Early concentrations of black Caribbean people were also present in Tampa, New Orleans, Boston, Cambridge, and Philadelphia, but most settled in New York City (Bryce-Laporte 1987).

Although the Caribbean had more direct access to Great Britain, its proximity to the United States made migration to this country a logical choice (Waters 1999). However, U.S. laws enacted over the years to regulate immigration determined the extent and intensity of the flow and subsequently created migratory waves with particular characteristics. The migration of black Caribbean people to the United States in the twentieth century can be divided into distinctive phases. The first wave began in the 1900s and climaxed between 1910 and 1925. Most of the émigrés during this time settled along the Eastern Seaboard, predominantly in New York City. Moreover, as a result of the immigration policies of the time, which used literacy as a criterion for immigration, many of these arrivals at the turn of the twentieth century were men and were exceptionally educated and skilled people who participated in the intellectual, political, and economic leadership of the city (Watkins-Owens 2001). Some argue that during this time, given their relatively small numbers, these early immigrants immersed themselves in the African American community and largely hid their "West Indian" and Caribbean heritage (Foner 2001).

In the 1920s the United States tried to restrict immigration from this region by enacting a quota system. However, as part of the British Commonwealth, black Caribbean people circumvented this policy by coming to the United States under the quota for Great Britain, which was substantially higher than that set for their own nations (Waters 1999). It was not until the onset of the Great Depression in the early 1930s that the number of black Caribbean people seeking entrance into the United States declined. During this period, even some who had already emigrated returned to their islands of origin. After World War II, black Caribbean immigration to the United States increased again. However, this flow was curbed by the McCarran-Walter Act of 1952, which prohibited colonial subjects from entering the United States under the quota of their colonizers, and reduced the quota of colonies to one hundred persons per year (Waters 1999).

In 1965 the United States implemented yet another reform of its immigration policies, catalyzing an era of black Caribbean migration that differed from other periods in history because of the volume of people who immigrated and the ensuing racial and political conflict into which they entered. On October 3, 1965, President Lyndon Johnson signed the Hart-Celler Immigration Bill, which phased out the national-origins quota system established in 1921. The new legislation valued family reunification and needed skills rather than immigrants' country of birth, supposedly allowing equal access to all peoples regardless of nationality (Center for Immigration Studies 1995).

The recruitment of workers centered on procuring two forms of labor—agricultural for the sugar fields and professional—and created a community of skilled as well as unskilled and poor constituents (Portes and Grosfoguel 1994). Jamaicans and other people from the English-speaking Caribbean were attractive to U.S. industries because they spoke English, making them ideal for service/personal service jobs. These immigrants were also perceived as coming from an advanced educational system that produced skilled workers, such as nurses, who were needed in the United States. The poor, rural farmers of the English-speaking Caribbean could also be recruited to work in sugar fields. In the last forty-five years, nurses and other health-care professionals have been especially recruited. However, as can be seen in the preceding historical review, professionals have been a part of black Caribbean migration to New York City since the early 1900s, giving black Caribbean peoples a different socioeconomic profile than that of other Caribbean immigrants and black Americans (Portes and Grosfoguel 1994).

The recruitment of workers to the United States—coupled with barriers against Commonwealth immigration erected by Britain in the 1960s—encouraged the migration of English-speaking Caribbean peoples to the United States, a trend that persists today. English-speaking Caribbean people continue to have a significant presence in the United States. Jamaica is one of the top fifteen immigrant-sending nations to the United States (U.S. Department of Homeland Security 2011), and an estimated 400,000 Guyanese, Trinidadians, and Jamaicans (the most prominent English-speaking Caribbean nationalities migrating to the United States) have made the United States their home (Rytina 2006). In 2011 approximately 32,878 persons from the Anglophone Caribbean obtained permanent residency in the United States, which is about 3.1 percent of all immigrants receiving green cards and over 9.5 percent of those coming from North America (U.S. Department of Homeland Security 2011).[4]

New York City, particularly the boroughs of Brooklyn, Queens, and the Bronx, hosts the largest concentration of English-speaking Caribbean immigrants in the nation (New York Department of City Planning 2013). With a population of more than half a million, this immigrant community is about five times the size of Grenada and twice the size of Barbados (U.S. Census Bureau 2010). When considered together, in 1998 immigrants from the Anglophone Caribbean constituted the largest immigrant group in the city (Foner 2001, 4). In fact, in 2001 immigrants from the English-speaking Caribbean between the ages of twenty-four and fifty-four comprised 58 percent of New York's black population (Mose Brown

2011, 25). Most Anglophone Caribbean émigrés settle in New York City because their people's migration to this metropolis, established early in the twentieth century, created an Anglophone Caribbean community in which many newcomers had some relatives or existing contacts (Waters 1999; Bryce-Laporte 1972). Furthermore, New York City's move toward a more service-oriented economy created jobs that English-speaking Caribbean people could fill.

Black Caribbean Diasporic Identity Studies

This book is informed by and builds on a growing body of literature on black Caribbean immigrant identity in general in the United States. The existing literature on the identity of first-generation diasporic black Caribbean peoples reflects three major themes, the most recurrent being black Caribbean people's encounters with and reactions to the form of racism cultivated in the United States. According to the literature, people from the black Caribbean hail from black-majority social and political systems with histories of black power movements (Waters 1999), nations where racial hierarchy is organized by color as well as shade (Sutton and Makiesky-Barrow 1987), and where education, income, and culture can partially overcome structural racism and "erase" blackness (Waters 1999; Foner 1998). This fact, combined with their status as voluntary immigrants, arguably makes black Caribbean immigrants experience and deal with race relations differently than their black American counterparts do. Furthermore, some scholars posit that even though black Caribbean people are cognizant of the racial structures of the United States before they enter the country (through media portrayals of America, stories from relatives and friends in the United States, and the immigrants' experiences in their own countries [Waters 1999; Foner 1998; Sutton and Makiesky-Barrow 1987]), they are often taken aback by overt racial discrimination (such as insults on the street and refusal to be employed) and more subtle forms of racism (such as being followed in stores).

The second theme in the literature pertains to black Caribbean people's enduring bonds to their homelands and subsequent maintenance of their national and regional identities in the United States. Joyce Bennett Justus (1983), for instance, found that black Caribbean people in Los Angeles knew how to negotiate U.S. culture and institutions, but they had no reason to fully assimilate into U.S. society. Thus, black Caribbean immigrants seemed to maintain their national and regional identity in the United States, creating an enduring bond to their homelands. On the other hand, Mary Waters (1999) found that most of her respondents had no desire to actually resettle in their islands, had little interest in the politics of their homelands, and used their citizenship to bring others to United States. Their futures were thus tied to the United States and not their islands of origin, challenging their position as multinational and transnational subjects. Nancy Foner (1997) found more hybridized cultural practices in her study of black Caribbean families in the diaspora. Her participants engaged in "creolization," fusing premigration beliefs and practices with new norms to construct familial relationships that differed from those of both the sending and the receiving countries.

The third major theme is black Caribbean people's oppositional relationship and disidentification with African Americans. Many scholars have highlighted that black Caribbean immigrants strictly distinguish themselves from African Americans as a form of image management. For instance, Justus (1983) asserts that black Caribbean people strived to protect their status as foreigners because they believed that submersion into American society meant being grouped with American blacks, who have a negative group image in the United States and who have limited access to the means of economic betterment for which black Caribbean people left their home. Similarly, according to Constance Sutton and Susan Makiesky-Barrow (1987), while being black in British society made black Caribbean people conspicuous, being racialized bodies in the United States translated into erasure, compelling them to insist on differentiation as a crucial tactic in resisting cultural eradication. Waters (1999) has also concluded that this group of immigrants tried to maintain a Caribbean identity to avoid racism and discrimination, a move that precluded collective challenge to inequalities. Christine Du Bois

(2000) further asserts that black Caribbean people tended to reject the American conception of race because of the historical legacy of the Caribbean that cultivated constructions of race and ethnicity dissimilar to those embedded in U.S. society, but also because they wanted to assuage the threat of low social status that plagued black Americans.

While the majority of research on black Caribbean immigrants in the United States has focused on first-generation immigrants, there has been some scholarship on the U.S.-born children of this group. Literature on these second-generation black Caribbean immigrants focuses predominantly on their racial and ethnic identity in the United States. For instance, Waters (2001) explored this theme in her study of black Caribbean high school students in New York City, arguing that their experiences with discrimination, the racial socialization they received from home, and the peers they kept informed how they reacted to American society and the identity they developed. Sherry-Ann Butterfield (2004) also addressed the issue of racial identification, demonstrating how second-generation black Caribbean immigrants are conscious of both their race and their ethnicity in their everyday lives.

Some of these studies have specifically addressed the construction of diasporic identity among women and girls in the black Caribbean diaspora. For example, Foner (1986) explored the sex roles of Jamaican women in New York and London. Tamara Mose Brown (2011) studied how black Caribbean child-care workers use public spaces such as parks and public libraries to negotiate the racial and class tensions in the gentrified neighborhoods in which they work and to create a collective space to socialize and participate in cultural expression. Oneka LaBennett (2011) has also examined black Caribbean female adolescents' identity formation and subject making through the use of popular culture. In my previous works, I have also explored first- and second-generation black Caribbean women's struggle for cultural citizenship in the United States and the manner in which their cultural heritage influences their engagement with and interpretation of mainstream media texts in the United States.

Looking at the black Caribbean diaspora through the prism of gender is important. Caribbean families, including those of black Caribbean people, are matrifocal, emphasizing relations to mothers and mothers' relatives so that networks are formed around women (Ho 1999). Furthermore, black Caribbean women, both historically and contemporarily, have been the agents who immigrate to the United States and maintain connections to their homelands through remittances, goods, and care for children left behind (discussed more fully in chapter 2). Given black Caribbean women's centrality to black Caribbean society, particularly migration and the formation of black Caribbean diasporas, their discourses and activities related to ideological and corporeal negotiations should be highlighted. Studying their negotiations of social and cultural ideologies in the United States illuminates the major challenges, trends, and discourses that emerge in their communities.

Not many scholars of the black Caribbean diasporic community have explicitly explored body politics in the black Caribbean diaspora, particularly the aesthetic ideologies that black Caribbean immigrant women bring to and encounter in their new home. One of the few studies on this subject is by LaBennett (2011), who explored the manner in which black Caribbean teenage girls and boys in Brooklyn, New York, negotiated the dominant ideals of beauty being promoted on the reality show *America's Next Top Model*. The current text pushes this work by LaBennett by considering how black Caribbean women in the United States engage with the "thick black woman" ideology that is perceived as central to black femininity and the implications it has for their body image as well as their social marginalization in the United States. In other words it brings into question the very foundation of black women's dominant body politics. Furthermore, the text examines negotiations of body politics that happen in both mediated and nonmediated contexts. It creates a fuller picture of how black Caribbean women construct their body politics and negotiate embodied cultural citizenship in their everyday lives.

Overall, *Romance with Voluptuousness* advances the work of scholars who study the English-speaking Caribbean diaspora by centering black women's bodies, the struggles (and victories) they encounter because of their body politics, and the discourses and practices they mobilize in their everyday lives to create embodied cultural citizenship in the United States. Through focus groups and interviews, I examine how first- and second-generation black Caribbean women use beauty discourses and practices to create self-esteem and self-confidence and to insert themselves into U.S. society in the face of dehumanizing, disenfranchising ideologies about their bodies. More specifically, I explore their engagement with the body shape and size expectations of the black Caribbean and how they negotiate the racist, neocolonial ideologies associated with that figure in the United States. I argue throughout the text that the manner in which these women negotiate beauty-society systems is a part of their larger struggle for visibility and well-being in the United States.

Studying Body Politics among Black Caribbean Women

The analysis that follows is based on information gathered from focus groups and interviews conducted between 2006 and 2014 with thirty-seven first- and second-generation English-speaking Caribbean women in the United States (twenty-three of the first generation and fourteen of the second generation). These qualitative methods are ideal for this project because of their generative nature and their ability to allow participants to have a relatively open discussion of the topic. This allows for the free flow of ideas and the emergence of topics that may not have been included in my initial research agenda (D. Morgan 1997). Having the women liberally discuss their cultural conception of body presentation and care also fosters more inductive, grounded analysis. More importantly, beauty ideals are produced and reproduced in communicative interactions. Interviews and focus groups help to re-create these contexts and are thus useful for examining how people explain, justify, and articulate viewpoints on body politics in their real lives.

I recruited participants primarily from New York City, which, as mentioned earlier, houses one of the largest black Caribbean diasporic communities in the world. The initial participants were recruited through vouching figures (Weiss 1994, 34)—that is, friends, relatives, and associates with access to a variety of black Caribbean women in New York City—who recommended and solicited their black Caribbean friends, associates, and business clients for the study. Subsequent participants were recruited through a "snowball sampling" technique, a chain-referral system that entails asking respondents to refer other participants for the research study, thus enabling access to diverse sections of the community.

Both first- and second-generation participants in the study are working- and middle-class women between the ages of nineteen and fifty-five. Most of them migrated from or have heritage in Jamaica (which is not surprising, since Jamaicans comprise the largest group of black Caribbean immigrants in the city [U.S. Census Bureau 2010]), but there are also women from other islands, including Antigua, Trinidad and Tobago, St. Vincent, and Barbados. All have completed at least a high school education, and some have completed or are pursuing college degrees and technical or professional training. Most of the women reside in communities with a prominently Anglophone Caribbean presence and have social networks composed predominantly of black Caribbean people. Furthermore, many of the participants still have relatives and friends "back home" with whom they keep in contact via the telephone and the Internet or to whom they send remittances in the form of money and material goods. The women themselves visit the Caribbean with varying levels of frequency, but most have no desire to move permanently to the islands. All the participants are culturally situated (because of skin tone, hair texture, etc.) and self-identify as black women.

The narratives from the participants are supplemented with information from my own experiences within the English-speaking Caribbean community in New York City. As an immigrant from Jamaica, I spent over fifteen (continuous) years in a major black Caribbean enclave in New York City, where I interacted with and observed black Caribbean family members, friends, and colleagues at social gatherings, hair salons, restaurants, and in classrooms. While being of black Caribbean heritage and living in the community does not automatically make me an authority on this group, my cultural position provides knowledge of and experience with the community and facilitates the opportunity for informal observations of and interactions with cultural traditions and texts; my position in the culture affords a level of access to the community that may not have been granted to researchers of other cultural backgrounds.

Conducting research on one's own community can be both rewarding and problematic. On the grounds of a shared cultural heritage, I may be allowed greater access than someone who would be deemed a cultural outsider, and so am able to see through both "serpent and eagle eyes" (Anzaldua 1987, 78), the view from above/outside and below/inside. On the other hand, I also realize that my "insider" position does not guarantee better knowledge claims or even complete access to the community (Stacey 1988; Gorelick 2003; Acker, Barry, and Esseveld 1991). I may fail to problematize or interrogate certain aspects of the participants' responses because of hyperfamiliarity; I could neglect to make inquires that an "outsider" would make because I have taken some knowledges for granted; or I could rely too much on my own experiences with the culture to interpret their experiences, dismissing or overlooking those that do not resonate with my own.

However, we have to move beyond this discussion of the advantages and dangers of studying one's community, which implicitly endorses the idea that different vantage points generate better knowledge claims. Rather, it is important to recognize that, far from being a monolithic whole, identities are constructed around several axes (of gender, race, culture, and class), any one of which renders researchers insiders or outsiders in a given context (Narayan 2003; Minh-Ha 1990; Anzaldua 1987). Even in my dealings with "my own people," there are contexts where we are "drawn closer" together and others where we are "thrust apart" (Narayan 2003, 291). This was evident in my research project when the number of years and legal citizenship in the United States, my particular black Caribbean accent, and even my body type influenced the rapport that I developed with the women as well as their comfort with talking to me. Therefore, my multiple identifications partially neutralized the utility of my so-called insider position in the research situation.

My experiences with this study also challenge popular ideas about the powerful researcher and her powerless subjects, an issue also raised by Ann Phoenix (2001). My position as an academic did not automatically shift the balance of power in my direction. In fact, in many situations my education status (or my "book-knowledge") marked me as less knowledgeable and therefore less powerful in the eyes of women who valued "street smarts" and a "hard core" attitude. Admittedly, power is firmly placed in my hands during the writing of this book, as I determine how the women are represented. Nevertheless, it is important to realize that power shifts between the researcher and her respondents throughout the research process.

Given my fluid identity categories that simultaneously concede and retract power in research situations, it is best to claim situated rather than better knowledge, to "admit the limits of [my] purview from [my particular position] . . . because from particular locations all understanding becomes subjectively based and forged through interactions within fields of power relations" (Narayan 2003, 296).

Furthermore, focusing on insider/outsider positions reinforces a false bifurcation between researcher and respondents that undermines the collaborative and mutually beneficial nature of ethnographic research. My interactions with the women throughout this project have made me question and analyze my own decisions pertaining to hair (to relax or go natural), my anxieties about my own body, and my general self-presentation.[5] Among these women, I have found similar experiences related to body image and beauty ideals that have helped to foster a form of community. During the interview sessions, the women and I laughed, complained, deconstructed, and encouraged. After the sessions (and still today), many women talk about the sessions as being therapeutic; they talk about how much fun they had, and eagerly volunteer to organize other sessions for me. These relationships and communities that are created through research are often obscured, belittled, and simplified by preoccupation with insider/outsider locations.

Plan of the Book

Romance with Voluptuousness is divided into five chapters. Chapter 2 explores the self-representation of first- and second-generation English-speaking black Caribbean women. These identity narratives are significant as they reveal how the women construct and position themselves in the United States in response to the various environments and ideologies they encounter in the country. These narratives also play a crucial role in shaping and framing the women's engagement with the "thick black woman" and the thin hegemony in their new home and their claiming of embodied cultural citizenship.

Chapter 3 focuses on a particular aspect of the women's self-presentation, specifically their engagement with voluptuousness. It explores the particular ways in which these women conceptualize and perform, imagine and enact the "thick black woman" ideal. It examines how the voluptuous body is articulated in the women's construction of beauty, how the women are socialized into this ideal, and the complexities and contradictions of living within the voluptuous regime. Moreover, the chapter explores the social, economic, and psychological dangers of performing that voluptuousness in the beauty hegemony that governs dominant American society. It highlights the extent to which the women's alignment with the voluptuous ideal exacerbates their marginalization in the United States. In other words, the chapter seeks to unearth the ways in which black Caribbean women's idealization of the "thick black woman" happens at the expense of their own well-being.

Chapter 4 examines how the women create embodied cultural citizenship in the United States. As black Caribbean women in the United States, their race, gender, nationality, and body aesthetics can significantly impact their participation in American society. However, they can develop alternative discourses that challenge the dominant ideology of thinness and the social realities it creates. This chapter highlights the discourses and actions that the participants deploy to construct a space within which they can negotiate hegemonic beauty discourses. It examines the strategies they use to counter and undermine the social, economic, and psychological marginalization they experience in the United States because of the multiplicative effect of their race, gender, nationality, and body aesthetic.

I conclude the text by reflecting on the corporeal (in)visibility of black Caribbean women in the United States and the possibilities for radical change created by their embodied resistance and their use of the "master's tools" to subvert colonialist discourses and practices (Lorde 2007). I also highlight the larger implications of the study in regard to understanding and theorizing immigrant black women's body politics in the United States and their overall diasporic experience.

2 CONSTRUCTING DIASPORIC IDENTITY
Black Caribbean Women's Self-
Representation and Cultural Citizenship

As proffered in the works of scholars such as Stuart Hall (1990), James
Clifford (1994), and Avtar Brah (2003), diasporic identities exist in a tem-
poral "third space" (Bhabha 1994, 53) where the original cultural influences
from the homeland and the new home are remade to create unique and
liminal phenomena. In this sense, diasporic identities are not simply moments on the assimilation-insulation continuum but rather ideological
spaces that are being continuously negotiated and remade in response to
discourses within the diasporic space as well as those from the countries
of origin. As I (and my colleague Maurice M. Hall) posit: "Diasporas . . .
cannot be perceived as perpetuating cultures that have been fossilized or
mummified. Rather, diasporic spaces have to be seen as actively producing new cultural practices and forms in which the traditions, values and
mores of original homelands are recast within the new cultural context,
and the dominant culture is reinterpreted to facilitate the practices from
home" (2012, 3).

Furthermore, diasporic identities are constructed through discourses
that immigrants create in response to their positions in their new homes;
these narratives reflect their changing lives, the loss (of social status, references, and meanings) experienced in the migration process, and the
adjustments they must make to facilitate successfully building a new life

in a new country. This chapter explores the identity narratives that black women of the English-speaking Caribbean develop in response to their lived experiences in the United States. It highlights the challenges they face in their new homes and the discursive strategies they engage in to create cultural citizenship. These narratives are significant, for they form the basis of the women's diasporic identities, how they conceive of and represent themselves in the United States. These identity discourses also inform the "creative revelation" strategies, discourses, and behaviors that help the women to negotiate the beauty hegemony they face in the United States. In other words, their identity narratives shape their embodied cultural citizenship. Given the centrality of their self-representation in challenging corporeal invisibility and marginalization, it is necessary to discuss the major characteristics of their identities in the United States.

Black Caribbean Women and Marginalization in the United States

Migration has been a perennial feature of the Anglophone Caribbean existence and one that distinguishes this region from others in the Western Hemisphere, where emigration is relatively recent. In spite of the issue of brain drain and other concerns associated with the departure of citizens, outward migration is seen from the Caribbean perspective not as a problem but as an institutionalized strategy for economic betterment (Chaney 1987). Women have been, and continue to be, significant players and participants in migration from the English-speaking Caribbean to the United States. They were a substantial part of the first wave of black Caribbean migration in the early 1900s and have been credited with the development and maintenance of black Caribbean communities in the United States. Though their ties to and responsibility for families made migration more complicated for them than for their male counterparts, they were often the first ones in a family to migrate and subsequently facilitated the emigration of others. Furthermore, more so than their male counterparts, who were perceived as more likely to "run off" with American women, the women were expected and trusted to send remittances and goods to help care for the family left behind. In this sense, then, they were expected to be in constant contact with their homelands, a practice that facilitated the construction and maintenance of transnational ties (Watkins-Owens 2001).

Contemporary black women from the English-speaking Caribbean continue to be the most likely to emigrate from their homelands to the United States, a decision made possible by the continued practice of child fostering and network migration. Their migration also remains very strategic and goal-oriented, with many of them coming to the United States to secure economic betterment for themselves and their families. They also continue to send money and barrels of American goods to their families in their homelands, fostering connections to their culture and creating transnational subjectivities that suspend complete acculturation and assimilation into the U.S. culture. Black Caribbean women (historically and contemporarily) clearly bear the responsibility for the economic support of their families in the United States as well as the islands, a responsibility that also permeates the second generation. Consequently, their diasporic experiences are centered around economic success in the United States. In fact, both first- and second-generation black Caribbean women embrace the idea of industriousness, hard work, and productivity—having a job—as a significant aspect of the black Caribbean diasporic identity. In other words, their success as immigrants is measured by their ability to earn money.

However, black English-speaking Caribbean women living in the United States do not exist in an ideological vacuum, and several intersecting factors limit their access to gainful employment and social mobility. These women function within interlocking axes of race, gender, and nation, systems that create complicated "outsider within" positions (Collins 1998). As raced and gendered bodies, they necessarily contend with the dominance of white male ideologies in the United States. As women from or with heritage in the global South, they also have to wrestle with imperialistic and ethnocentric American ideologies. Their experiences are thus shaped by the multiplicative effect of being black women from developing countries.

These women face a particular form of American racism. The English-speaking Caribbean is often falsely perceived as a space of racial egalitarianism. Racism, or at least "white ethnocentrism" (Bryce-Laporte 1972, 40), exists in most of the countries from which black Caribbean immigrants come to the United States. It often manifests itself differently and may have a different order of importance, but societies of the black English-speaking Caribbean have a history of struggle with racial inequalities and white supremacy. In fact, the venerated black empowerment movements of the postcolonial, independence era in the Caribbean were not uncontested. Scholars such as Maziki Thame (2011a) and Anthony Bogues (2002) have illustrated how that movement in Jamaica, for example, was marginalized, co-opted, and suppressed by the brown or Creole power movement in the newly formed state.

Black Caribbean women migrating to the United States in the post–civil rights era are thus not experiencing racial structures and hierarchies for the first time when they enter the country; they are well aware of racial inequalities fostered by classic racism (overt exclusion and discrimination) as well as the newer, modern iteration that Eduardo Bonilla-Silva (2006) refers to as color-blind racism or the ideology of color blindness. This "new racism," he argues, was developed by whites to explain the overt contradiction between America's professed evolution into a society in which race is no longer relevant and its continued race-coded inequality. The ideology of color blindness explains this racial inequality in nonracial terms, drawing on frames of abstract liberalism (such as equal opportunity and individualism), "naturally occurring" phenomena, culturally based arguments, and the minimization of racism. These ideologies function to maintain the contemporary racial structure through subtle, institutional practices and help to underscore white privilege without incriminating whites (Bonilla-Silva 2006).

Indeed, color-blind racism has been a central feature of the racial landscape in the Caribbean since independence and operates similarly in the Caribbean (and Latin America) as it does in the United States. Many countries in this region pride themselves on being multiracial and multicultural and uphold ideologies of racial democracy. Jamaica, for example, codifies notions of its multiracialism in its motto, "Out of Many One People" (Thame 2011a). In most of these countries, however, the majority of the black population remains marginalized and disenfranchised and occupies lower socioeconomic positions than their white and brown counterparts. However, similar to the color-blind racial structure in the United States, these inequalities are attributed not to race but to other factors, such as cultural difference, the inherent laziness of black people, and class warfare. As Roy Bryce-Laporte writes: "It is simply untrue that the average black immigrant has come out of a nonracist situation. . . . In many of these countries, the white or lighter-skinned elite has capitalized on the myth of no racial problem. . . . Lower- and middle-class citizens of such countries come to accept this myth, which on one hand is ego-inflating and perhaps self-fulfilling, but, on the other, is the basis of a vicious, self-defeating trap which prevents them from responding to subtle racist abuses directly or publicly lest they be considered racist and unpatriotic" (1972, 39).

In this sense, black Caribbean women in the United States encounter a racial order similar to that of the Caribbean, one that ostensibly marginalizes them because of their race but explains its effects as the result of their culture and their choices. In other words, though they face institutionalized structures that marginalize them based on race, they have to contend with being blamed for their inability to advance in society and their lower social and economic status.

While color-blind racialism is not new to black Caribbean immigrant women, what I argue is new for them is their positioning in the U.S. racial hierarchy. In the context of dominant American society, their social and cultural capital (such as education and class privileges) are nullified and erased, their race is made more salient than their cultural identity, and they are required to take on the sole essentialized category of "black." Moreover, their heritage in the Caribbean further justifies or underscores the use of culturally based arguments ("cultural racism" [Bonilla-Silva 2006]) to explain their social and economic positions. Though much work has been done to debunk the exoticized images of people from the Caribbean, these women routinely encounter ethnocentric ideologies that label them as intellectually inferior, socially unsophisticated, and culturally backward. Ultimately, they are perceived as poor, dependent, and unprogressive, different from and inferior to their (black and white) American counterparts. I believe this existing ethnocentrism and Euro-American privilege make them more susceptible to cultural racism: it is more difficult for them to highlight and legitimize institutional racism when their cultures are perceived as "problematic" and as the root of their differential experiences. Their marginalization is more easily seen as a result of their cultural heritage and their socialization, and not the systematic racial structures of the United States.

Furthermore, the ethnocentric racialization strategies that black Caribbean women encounter track them into low-income neighborhoods, low-paying jobs, and general downward mobility (Waters 1999; Du Bois 2000; Gentles-Peart 2009a). Many black Caribbean women (both first and second generation), at least for a time, work as low-paid child-care workers and domestics, making it possible for white women to have careers, and filling the gap created by African American women leaving such work (Mose Brown 2011). Black Caribbean women also have a prominent presence in the lower tiers of the health-care sector of New York City, working as home health aides and nursing-home assistants (Sutton and Makiesky-Barrow 1987). Such "ethnic niching" (Model 2001), or the concentration of black Caribbean women in the personal and professional service industries, may be produced by several social factors. First, it is the direct result of U.S. immigration policies that provide visas for these women to function as child-care providers, nurses, and other health-care professionals in the United States. This phenomenon may also be the result of the émigrés' reliance on networks of family and friends who recommend and encourage entrance into their fields of work. Finally, their "niching" may be the effect of occupational discrimination that channels this group of immigrants toward the service industry. Whatever the reason, the historical and contemporary overrepresentation of black Caribbean women in the domestic and health-care sectors reinforces the stereotype of them as service workers, a perception that has found prolific expression in U.S. media, and one that they must contend with in the United States.

Within their community, the women in this study are very candid about their experiences with discrimination and micro-aggressions in the United States. Many of these accounts are from child-care workers and nannies who describe interactions with white employers that demonstrate the effect of the intersection of class and race on their experiences in white, upper-middle-class environments. They describe situations in which they are routinely ignored and disregarded, made to feel invisible by their employers and friends of employers who do not acknowledge or greet them and who refuse to speak to them on the phone. They recount feeling infantilized by how their employers try to control and manage their schedules, and how their employers habitually intrude and make demands on their time and lives. One of the most poignant accounts is from Charlotte, a former paralegal who was then employed as a nanny:[1] "Some will say hi to you . . . and others will just totally disregard you. They will look right through you like you transparent or something. . . . They feel that they are superior to you because of the color of their skin. Like even when they would call the house . . . some of them would not choose to give me a message, and tell me if I could hang up and they'll call back and let the answering machine pick up, or if they are calling out something for me, they want me to repeat." Tamara Mose Brown (2011) reports similar sentiments from the black Caribbean nannies in her study, who also had to contend with racial and class tensions in the gentrified neighborhoods of Brooklyn in which they worked.

Women in other sectors of the U.S. work force also share numerous accounts of experiences with African American and Caucasian colleagues. They talk about the derision and marginalization they encounter from both black and white coworkers in New York City because of their nationality. They discuss being perceived as primitive because they are from or have heritage in the Caribbean, and having to contend with questions and comments that imply that they are simple, that coming to the United

States is an automatically upwardly mobile move, and that Americans are therefore better than they are. For example, Wilma shares her confrontations with African American colleagues:

> While I was a supervisor at that store, this one African American guy said to me, "Before you came here you didn't know what Levis jeans were." . . . He thought that me being here was the first time that I got to see clothes and shoes and know what food is. I thought that was so ignorant. I was better off back home than he is here. This one other guy asked, "Do you live in a hut?" He thought that I lived in a hut. . . . All these stupid comments like, "Do you have TV back there?" I'm like, "Does he even read?"

Her sister, Lily, similarly comments on African American ethnocentrism. She says, "In terms of [African American women's] black consciousness, I think that they think of themselves as superior to us, to blacks in the Caribbean. They look at us as if we don't know what they know."

The women's skills and education are often devalued and undermined because of their race, gender, and heritage, which, particularly for the first generation, results in downward mobility and settling for previously unacceptable living arrangements. This is a point of anxiety for many women in the community who mourn the loss of the economic and social positions they occupied in their homelands. The women who attended primary and secondary educational institutions in the United States (such as those of the second generation or those who migrated as children) experienced Eurocentrism and racism from educators as well as peers. A common narrative is of being "held back" or being placed in a lower grade when matriculated in their schools because of the perceived inferiority of the education they received in the islands. Equally commonplace are stories of being teased and ostracized in school because of the pronunciation and cadence they had learned in black Caribbean households. A couple of women even speak about being subjected to remedial speech therapy to "correct" their accents.

While the women's accounts are commonplace in black Caribbean communities, they are obscured and contradicted in dominant society by narratives of black Caribbean women's exemplary characteristics. In American and Western consciousness, black Caribbean women, by virtue of their heritage, are perceived as intellectually inferior (as discussed earlier) but also as good workers (that is, hardworking, loyal, caring, trustworthy, and happy to serve). Some have even referred to black Caribbean immigrants overall as a form of "model minority," a meritocratic designation that assumes the community is overwhelmingly successful and attributes its perceived triumph over poverty and disruption of migration to the immigrants' own hard work. Indeed, the black Caribbean culture has been extolled as promoting hard work, saving, and investment and is thus upheld as superior to other black ethnicities such as African American (Glazer and Moynihan 1963).

However, this does not reflect the overall reality of black Caribbean people, who generally are employed in the service sectors of New York City and live in the less wealthy areas of the city (Hintzen 2001). Furthermore, this narrative does not reflect the women's own reports of how they are treated in the workforce and mainstream society in general. Therefore, black Caribbeanness for them differs from popular Eurocentric constructs in the United States. For real women in the community, their connections to the Caribbean, a "third world" space in current geopolitics, concurrently marks them as hardworking but unsophisticated, caring but infantile, fun-loving but ignorant, poor but happy—a dialectic that they must contend with in their everyday lives. Therefore, as Percy Hintzen (2001) observes, the rhetoric of black Caribbean people as a model minority is more related to the politics of race relations in the United States (that is, the further marginalization of African Americans in American society) than to the actual lives of black Caribbean people.

Black Caribbean women are also "symbolically annihilated" by American mainstream media (Tuchman 1978, 3). They rarely appear in media, and when they do, they are depicted paradoxically as overly sexual dancehall queens and self-sacrificing nannies and loving nurses, the Venus and the Mammy. In fact, black Caribbean people in general are represented negatively in American media. In his textual analysis of black Caribbean characters in American films, Milton Vickerman (1999) found that black Caribbean peoples were usually depicted in three distinct, stereotypical ways depending on the genre: they were portrayed contradictorily as beauty and danger in films about tourists, plantations, and horrors; as buffoons in comedies; and as immigrant, criminal elements in movies with a prominent Rastafari presence. Analogously, in her book titled *Images of West Indians in the Mass Media*, Christine Du Bois (2004) highlights seven themes that have pervaded representations of black Caribbean people in films, including rebels, jokesters, and overly sexual islanders. Furthermore, she also found that the news media in the Chesapeake area, when they did address this population, predominantly presented black Caribbean people as criminals. However, advertising in the area chose to emphasize a different image when addressing the nonblack Caribbean population. They marketed black Caribbean people as symbols of pleasure, as carefree, fun-loving "others" from distant paradises, and they appropriated aspects of black Caribbean culture (such as music) to attract Americans to the isles.

Black Caribbean women encounter these "controlling images" (Collins 1998) in their everyday lives. The American mainstream media do not necessarily create these discourses about black Caribbean people in general and women in particular, but they do help to circulate them. Relatedly, media in the United States do not *make* individuals believe a particular idea or act in certain ways. However, media do help normalize ideas, making them seem like common sense or natural and thus making them more difficult to resist and challenge (Gerbner and Gross 1976). Moreover, media create an environment where it is normal to treat people differentially based on these ideas. For instance, by continuously presenting black Caribbean women as dance-hall queens and nannies, American media help to solidify the perception that real black Caribbean women are hypersexual and not capable of functioning in professional, nondomestic settings. They also justify and support the marginalization of these women in American spaces. The ideological and material challenges created by racism and ethnocentrism and normalized by media representations characterize the lives of working-class and lower-middle-class black Caribbean women living in New York City, and necessarily inform the ways in which they talk about and present themselves in their diasporic space. In other words, their experiences with racism, sexism, classism, and Eurocentrism inform the construction of their diasporic identities.

Scholars have found that displaced peoples develop identities in response to the particular diasporic spaces that they occupy and as a means of contending with the distress of the resettlement process. For instance, in her study of Senegalese men in southern Italy, Dorothy Zinn (2005) found that her respondents used the trope of world traveling to describe their migration experience, a move that allowed them to discuss their harsh circumstances as phases in the development of manhood and the acquisition of international knowledge and experience. In doing so, the men justified to themselves that their migration was not in vain, even if they returned materially empty-handed to Senegal (Zinn 1994). Analogously, Gadi Ben-Ezer (2002) reported that Ethiopian Jews imbued their migration to Israel with religious significance. Though marginalization and persecution prompted them to leave Ethiopia, they attributed the time of departure to the time being "right" as decided by God. Many of the events they encountered were interpreted as God's guidance, intervention, and help. They also drew parallels between the hardships of their actual migration and what the Children of Israel endured in their journey to the promised land, a process that God used to purge the unrighteous; the Ethiopians' successful entrance into Israel was a sign of their righteousness and deservedness to enter their promised land (Ben-Ezer 2002).

Black English-speaking Caribbean women engage in similar discursive work. They develop identity narratives as strategies to negotiate the challenges they face in the United States. In this way, they construct their identities to create cultural citizenship, spaces of inclusion, and recognition within U.S. society and culture; they construct identity narratives to create an acceptable life in the diaspora.

First-Generation Identity Narratives: The Permanent Foreigners

My years of research and engagement with the community reveal that the self-representation of first-generation black Caribbean women in New York City (that is, those who were born and predominantly raised in the Caribbean) is largely characterized by claiming difference from and dis-identification with all Americans and others in their diasporic space; they discursively establish a permanent foreigner status. These observations reflect and confirm what others have found in relation to black Caribbean people in general. However, my analysis expands current literature by exploring these discourses of difference through the prism of gender. I explore the ways in which women create and maintain the permanent foreigner status. I provide insight into the values that first-generation working-class and lower-middle-class women of the community prioritize and foreground in their diasporic subjectivities and highlight how they construct their identities around the notion of difference. My observations also reveal the lens through which first-generation women of the community interpret American society, the standards they use to judge its quality, and how they make sense of their experiences in the United States.

Generally, the women perceive themselves as different from and superior to both black and white Americans in three specific areas. While conceding that the United States has a better economy and "stronger dollar," the women find American values deficient compared to those cultivated in their islands, particularly as related to education, discipline, and work ethic. They believe the prominence of education in their culture engenders students who are more focused and dedicated than African Americans and white Americans. According to Wilma, who had to work as a full-time waitress to pay her tuition, "Americans here have everything; they get to go to school at any age. They can get financial aid and go to school for free, yet they won't. And the Dominicans I know are very goal-driven because education is so important to them." Katherine implicitly concurs with her counterpart, commenting: "I know I'm here to go to school, but there are so many other things, so many parties you could go to, so many other things you get involved in that could pull you away from that.... Just coming from where you're from, and being raised the way you're raised, I think [makes you steady]."

Both women believe that, unlike "their people," for whom erudition is tantamount, Americans squander their educational privilege, neglecting to avail themselves of the myriad academic opportunities in the United States and failing to appreciate what is available to them. They contend that their cultural heritage equips them to remain focused in spite of the distractions present in the United States, diversions that may and do cause people with less solid foundations—that is, Americans—to deviate from their goals.

The women are also convinced that people raised in the Caribbean or by black Caribbean parents are more disciplined than their American counterparts, know how to conduct themselves in public, and show appropriate respect to everyone. In response to my question about the types of values that characterize Americans, Charlotte quips, "Are there any values in America? Really. I mean take for example the way Americans discipline their kids. You would see like a five-year-old telling [her] mother to shut up, or the parent would ask them to do something and they wouldn't do it. I couldn't dare do that in St. Lucia, or any island for that matter. I'm thirty-six, I live on my own, I'm married, and I am so careful what I say to my mother because of the level of respect I have for [my] mother." Her irritation is directed toward some African Americans but mostly toward upper-middle-class white women with whom she interacts on her job as a nanny. She claims that they make excuses for their children instead of punishing their bad behavior. Her statement is a critique of American behavior but more specifically an indictment of the parenting capabilities of white Americans; Charlotte perceives black Caribbean women as better mothers who raise respectful, well-behaved children.

Margerie expresses this sentiment more overtly:

I take care of two little kids, and I teach them the same thing that I was taught. So the older boy he goes out, and everybody sees him, and they [say], "Margerie, what did you do to this child? I mean he is so different." I mean, he has friends coming over, they look at me in my eye. . . . They don't even greet me or say, "Hi" or anything. He's not like that. . . . He meets their parents, [he says], "Hi, Mrs. so and so, and Mr. so and so," and "Nice to meet you." If my friend comes over too, he shakes their hands.

Like Charlotte, Margerie works as a nanny taking care of upper-middle-class white American boys. She believes that it is only through her association with them that they can develop appropriate respect; she passes on to them what she was taught in Dominica and thus creates respectful and disciplined children, regardless of their racial background. The fact that the difference is evident to white Americans and they inquire about the techniques that she uses to produce such behavior suggest to her that such capabilities and traits elude her white counterparts. Not greeting her and neglecting to acknowledge her presence are certainly indicative of racial and class-based issues, but Margerie interprets these behaviors as the result of the bad mothering fostered in the American society and uses this experience to claim difference from (and superiority over) white Americans.

Likewise, the women allege that, having had to work all their lives, they are better and harder workers compared to African Americans, who they believe are too hasty to accept welfare. Jamie says: "They said that these Jamaicans they come here and they take away other people's jobs. My response to that was if you wanted the jobs we wouldn't be able to come here and get any. So what does that say about you? You don't want to work and we want to work so we work six jobs." Having six jobs may have been an exaggeration (informed by dominant popular stereotypes of black Caribbean people as holding many jobs), but it is illustrative of her point. For her, the fact that Jamaicans are able to get the jobs of African Americans is a demonstration of the latter's complacency, particularly when compared to black Caribbean people, who are theoretically willing to hold six.

Cassie also states, "I'm thinking right now of two American black women that were actually born in the north up here. One I end up firing because she was not doing her job. . . . So I go through this stuff with this person, and they just not doing their job. . . . I actually found that after I terminated her that she [got] caught back in drugs." Donna also observes, "From what I've seen, there's a huge difference where work ethic is concerned. I think we take so much pride in ourselves that we'll have second thoughts when it comes to going on certain welfare programs or just [government checks] or anything like that, and it's the first thing [that] jump into [African American's] mind, as far as I am concerned. . . . We've always worked, in one way or another. West Indians, from my experience, have always been working, always been expected to work." Gainful employment is a proud part of these women's identity, a feature that they think is inherently lacking in African Americans. Their (limited) experiences reaffirm the perceived character flaw of the African American women in New York City, who reportedly have a bad work ethic, rely on government assistance, and are prone to drug use.

Equally vexing for the women is the lack of work ethic among white Americans. Donna asserts, "The most experience I've had with white people are white Jewish people who come from money, and to me, there's no [similarity between us] because they don't have to necessarily work. Their parents already work and have stuff provided for them to do their education and then from there, they start their own life. And I realize that coming from Jamaica I have to work to pay my way through school." In other words, white Americans are always already privileged and do not have to hold jobs. While her tone indicates her resentment toward this group of wealthy white Americans, she does not perceive them as better than their African American counterparts where work ethic is concerned; white Americans' economic privilege fosters a lack of work ethic that is similar to that of African Americans.

The Accent as Difference

The discourse of difference is also manifested in the women's discussion of their accents. They believe that their particular inflections and enunciations are major manifestations of their black Caribbean and national identities, the symbol and expression of their cultural heritage in the United States. Brenda says: "I feel like having this accent is a part of who I am. To me it goes way back." Charlotte also recounts: "One time I was talking to my girlfriend back home and she said she heard a little American twang. I said, 'I'm a Lucian; never forget that. I'd never get rid of that accent.'" By speaking of remaining St. Lucian and retaining her accent in the same statement, this participant indicates that she sees the preservation of her accent as representative of her connection to her nation, conflating the presence of her accent with her national and cultural identity. Ingrid's response at least partially provides the explanation for Charlotte's insistence on the retention of her accent. When asked why it is important for her to preserve her own accent, Ingrid vehemently states, "I don't want to lose my accent cause that's the only thing I have from my country. That's the only thing that would stay on me. I could always represent my country by my accent, cause we can't dress in our flag color and stuff like that, so it's only your accent you have. . . . That's all you have." Her accent is thus the public, readily noticeable aspect of her cultural identity, which, similar to a national flag, identifies her to others as St. Lucian. For these women, accents are organic and naturally emanate from a cultural center.

More importantly, their accents are the ultimate signifier of difference. Evelyn explains, "The accent was gone. . . . I adopted so much of the American culture. . . . [When I went back to visit at fifteen, I found Jamaica.] I realized how beautiful Jamaica is, and, I'm telling you, I never lost it. The accent was never lost. Once I went back to Jamaica and found it again, for some reason now the American accent was gone for good. I never got it back." In other words, her accent represents her connection to her homeland and her simultaneous distance from and lack of adaptation of the American culture. The salience of her accent is a reflection of her Jamaicanness and un-Americanness. As Ingrid says: "Even at work when I make certain calls, people would say, 'Where're you from?' And I would say, 'St. Lucia,' and they say, 'True? I love your accent,' and stuff like that. The only thing, I don't want nobody to tell me that I sound like an

American cause I don't. I don't. I love my St. Lucian accent." Her comment reveals that, to her delight, her accent amplifies and makes conspicuous her difference and "foreign" status.

These comments demonstrate that the women employ inflections and enunciations to express their cultural identity and establish difference from Americans. Note that their desire to maintain their distinctive accents is not borne from their hope of returning to their homelands, as most of the women do not have plans to resettle in the Caribbean. Rather, the women's determination to preserve their accents is directly related to their decision to live in the United States and their position as immigrants in the country: while in the United States, they do not want to lose their black Caribbean inflections and thus their black Caribbean identity to the American culture, a culture that marginalizes them and undermines their value as subjects and citizens. Therefore, black Caribbean women's accents not only serve as cultural identification in the United States but also mark them as a perpetual "other" and locate their identity outside the United States. In this way, then, the preservation of their accents allows first-generation black Caribbean women to resist full assimilation into the American culture and undermines the "melting pot" ideology that pervades immigration discourses in the United States (Hintzen 2001, 164; Gentles-Peart 2014).

As discussed in chapter 1, some scholars attribute this distancing to black Caribbean immigrants' attempts to minimize racism and attain prominence in a society that renders invisible people of their race and culture. Race is undoubtedly a major factor in understanding the prominence of difference in the first-generation women's identity discourse. However, I reflect differently on the women's permanent foreigner status. The overreliance on race and racial identification as the main explanatory framework for black Caribbean diasporic identity undermines the significance of transnational realities in its formation; it simplifies and flattens the complex positionalities that characterize the experiences of black Caribbean women residing in the United States. These women function within interlocking axes of race, gender, and nation, systems that create complicated "outsider within" positions (Collins 1998). In other words, they concurrently negotiate racism, sexism, *and* Eurocentrism. By foregrounding only race in the interpretation of black Caribbean people's distinction from Americans, we impose a very American-centric paradigm that ignores the postcolonial and neocolonial dimensions of their realities and their implications for black Caribbean women's diasporic discourses in the United States.

Relatedly, the extant rationalizations do not take into account the realities of migration and relocation that compel these immigrants to construct such an identity in the United States. The narrative of difference is a cognitive strategy employed by first-generation Caribbean women to confront and assuage the challenges they encounter in New York City as low- and lower-middle-income black women from developing countries and to negotiate the multiplicative effect of gender, race, class, and coloniality. This becomes evident when we consider the instances and situations within which the women mobilize the narrative of difference. For instance, some of the respondents deploy the notion of difference in values in the context of their encounters with affluent white Americans. Margerie, the Bronx-based nanny who prides herself on her autonomy, says with disdain, "Because of the job that I do, that's how I get to interact with [white women] so most of them are mothers who don't work; the husband taking care of stuff, so they [stay] home. . . . As far as independent, they depend on their husbands, I don't; I depend on me, even if I have a husband . . . I take care of my own. So I don't think I have anything in common with them." Margerie does not interpret the situation from a socioeconomic perspective, seeing her employer's ability to stay home as reflective of the high income status of a household that does not need two incomes to sustain it, thus making the wife's employment optional. Instead, she attributes her employer's decision to stay home and concede financial responsibility for the home to her husband as a clear difference in morals and values. For her, a woman who prides herself as being a hard worker, such choices are indicative of a lack of self-reliance and self-respect; even with the presence of a man who could "take care of stuff," she will never relinquish her independence to anyone.

Similarly, Lorna, a young woman from Barbados, speaks incredulously about the extensive vacations taken by some of her white counterparts. She comments: "Mostly Caucasian people that I know . . . they say that after high school they took a year off, and they went to wherever. I guess I would like to do that. I probably could, but I don't know if I would want to. . . . That's one of the . . . cultural difference[s]. [West Indian] people are encouraged to be more. . . . That's one of the differences." Lorna implicitly defines herself as a serious student, whose goal is to finish her undergraduate studies, immediately go on to get her master's degree, and start her career. She thus views traveling for such long periods before accomplishing her academic goals as unfocused and distracting, an activity that she says she has no desire to partake in. However, world traveling is a middle- to upper-middle-class phenomenon because only a relatively small percentage of Americans can afford such a luxury, a point that the participant does not mention in her reflection. In a situation where her class status is made salient, she interprets it as a difference in cultural values.

Carol also speaks about her experiences with the rich, white people of Long Island:

> You'd hear them in their little clusters. . . . This one would be talking about what camp his son is going to, and this one would be talking about this. . . . Nothing that pertains to me, and nothing that I cared for anyway. And I felt a little uneasy or like an outcast I guess, and then I told my boss about it. I tell her, "Listen, I don't wanna go there any more." So then she was saying [I] have to learn to deal with people. I said, "I don't need to deal with them," . . . and then I just stop going. I don't put myself in that situation. It's a very uncomfortable situation.

According to this candid statement, her feeling like an outcast is not related to the fact that she was the black nanny among wealthy white people but rather because she had no interest in those topics, which she deems indulgent. She attributes her discomfort to irreconcilable differences in cultural interests and not due to the blatant class (and racial) inequality.

In this way, when confronted with the affluence of white Americans, the women do not acknowledge their low class position. Rather, in these moments, the respondents dismiss the overt economic discrepancies as differences in cultural tastes and values. Recasting the luxuries associated with wealth as matters of bad taste and cultural deficiency allows the women to create a space of empowerment; while it does not dismantle the race and class hierarchies, it does allow them to claim moral superiority (and power) over the wealthy white American women they encounter in their lives.

Employing the discourse of differences in priorities also allows the participants to invert practices of exclusion and belonging and take an empowered stance in relation to wealth and class in the United States: their relatively low-paying jobs, their working-class neighborhoods, and their relative lack of material prosperity are all indicative of their marginalization from the "American Dream." However, rather than reverencing and showing deference to the wealthy, which would signify acceptance of their own economic lack, the women deploy discourses to reject the trappings of the "American Dream." In this way, they are not excluded from the spaces and activities of the wealthy, but rather they do not desire inclusion and thus create a space where those things are marginalized.

Overall, these identity narratives of difference in values are problematic. First, the use of cultural difference to interpret wealth gaps is flawed, for it allows the women to avoid confronting the economic inequalities and incongruities that exist between them and affluent white Americans, and it foregoes exposing the structures that uphold them. It therefore forestalls challenging the status quo and leaves the racial and economic hierarchy intact. Discourses of difference and superiority also reflect the general schema used to categorize black Caribbean immigrants in the United States as a "model minority" and to foster ethic tensions among immigrant blacks and African Americans (Hintzen 2001). Furthermore, while some of the participants' impressions of American blacks and whites are derived from a few personal interactions with members of these groups, their limited experience and contact with either group indicate that the material used in the construction of their perceptions is gathered through indirect means, most notably, the media. In fact, the participants' conception of Anglo and African Americans conspicuously reflect the stereotypical image of these groups propagated by mainstream media. The black welfare queen, the party-loving college students, and the way that race is generally used as an indicator of class are ubiquitous in prime-time news and television drama series, which they admit to watching extensively. In other words, American popular culture cultivates the women's impressions of and attitudes toward black and white Americans. In this way, the women's discourse of superiority rehearses and reinforces the racist and elitist ideologies of their new home.

On the other hand, rather than creating American subjects, popular culture gives these women the material necessary to claim superiority over Americans in their own country. Black Caribbean women's discourse of superiority is an explicit challenge to and rejection of the derision and marginalization they face in New York City. These women create an affirming identity to help them survive in this milieu; they tell the narrative of superiority about themselves to themselves and others in order to deal with the prejudices they face. Dominant discourses and, to a lesser extent, personal experience aid in the formation of such narratives, demonstrating that far from being passive, the "'margins' do imagine and construct the 'mainstream' in order to assert superiority over it" (Espiritu 2001, 416).

Second-Generation Identity Narratives: Flexible Citizenship

While the first-generation women construct a permanent foreigner identity, the self-representations of second-generation black Caribbean women are characterized by liminality. As part of the second generation, these women have a connection to the Caribbean and the United States that differs from that of their first-generation counterparts. For one, they are natural-born (not naturalized) citizens of the United States, an empire in the developed world. Additionally, they were raised in Caribbean homes but not in the Caribbean and thus have some level of physical and cultural separation from the "third world." Furthermore, while born in the United States and socialized in the black Caribbean culture, neither the Caribbean nor the United States is fully their home. Thus, their identity narratives derive from a culturally hybrid existence and the condition of straddling two worlds. Because of this, they have access to discourses and liberties not available to previous generations, which allows them to cultivate complex hybrid identities.

Specifically, these women claim legal (American) citizenship and cultural (black Caribbean) nationhood; they are legally Americans but culturally black Caribbean women. They are citizens of the United States and have American passports, but they generally distance themselves from American culture and people, at least rhetorically, and locate themselves within the black Caribbean "nation."[2] To do this, they construct a clear distinction between black Caribbean and American ontologies similar to that created by their first-generation counterparts. In relation to social behavior and cultural norms, they characterize Americans as "crazy," disrespectful, untidy, materialistic, a-cultural and generally unfriendly. Karrie says: "Just [American] facial expressions alone! Sometimes you say good morning, and they're looking at you like why are you talking to me. . . . I don't know if it's an American thing, like you're afraid to talk to strangers, whereas with Jamaicans, they're just open and free." Black Caribbean people, on the other hand, are disciplined, hardworking, respectful, and "laid back." They value education, being polite, being tidy and clean, and showing deference to elders and people in authority.

This characterization of black Caribbean people as having better morals and civility than Americans echoes those presented by the first-generation women. Clearly, these narratives are a significant part of black Caribbean women's identity in the diaspora and are widely rehearsed and disseminated within their communities. The second-generation women iterate them here and explicitly align themselves with these ideas of Caribbeanness. Tamara explains: "I'm an American citizen because I was born here, but I don't think it makes me American because of the household that I live in. . . . Because my family is Jamaican, it makes me more closer to the Caribbean culture." Tony also says: "I'm so used to the whole Jamaican environment; I grew up with it so I just feel like that's me. I am Jamaican; nobody can tell me [differently]. I know I was born here, but I am Jamaican in the blood." For both women, their black Caribbean upbringing gives them an ontological orientation that is distinct from that of Americans, thus making them more aligned with the black Caribbean "nation." Another participant, Debbie, overtly says: "You can call me Trinidadian, you can call me West Indian, but if you call me American, we are going to have problems." Brenda similarly says that she reluctantly identifies as American when she visits Grenada, her mother's island, but this is only because the "locals" can tell that she is not from there. In other words, she only identifies as a non-Grenadian in relation to people who are "fully" Grenadians.

By resisting being called American and self-identifying as black Caribbean women, the women situate their identity in their cultural orientation and ontology rather than their geographic place of birth. In this way, they distinguish between citizenship and nationhood, between a sense of belonging that is bestowed (usually by a polity) and one that is claimed on the basis of a shared culture and ontology. They also challenge dominant discourses of statehood that perpetuate the idea of a singular culture or "nation" within a country and the myth of a monolithic nationalism (Bogues 2002; Strelitz 2004). However, their subjectivities are much more complicated and dialectic than their cultural self-identity implies. Their Caribbean and American identities are not static, mutually exclusive categories; rather, the women move fluidly between the two based on specific contexts and the perceived personal benefits to be achieved. Specifically, the women construct *flexible identities*; they claim a black Caribbean cultural identity but frequently align themselves with the United States when it proves personally beneficial to them.

According to Aihwa Ong, "flexible citizenship" refers to the strategies used by diasporic subjects to bypass and benefit from different nation-states so as to maximize capital accumulation; it entails "complex maneuvers that subvert reigning notions of national self and the Other in transnational relations" (1999, 112). Therefore, rather than embracing citizenship based on allegiance to country of birth, immigrants negotiate their citizenship based on economic factors. Second-generation black Caribbean women also engage in similar tactics: while they are neither transnationally mobile nor economic elites, as Ong's Asian professionals, they seem to biculturally construct their subjectivities in order to strategically position themselves in the United States and subsequently take advantage of social and economic opportunities. In this way, they have *flexible identities*.

This flexible identity is facilitated by the liminal consciousness cultivated by their fractured relationship with the United States and the English-speaking Caribbean. In the first place, they are stigmatized in the United States because of their race and cultural heritage, a reality that belies their noncitizen status, despite the fact that they are born in the United States. As with other black and brown ethnic communities in the United States, they are subjected to marginalization on the basis of race, gender, and ethnicity, and they are denied economic and social mobility. Being marginalized in the country of their birth undermines their sense of belonging. They are not accepted as "real" Americans, so it is not surprising that they disassociate themselves from the people and culture that refuse to acknowledge them.

On the other hand, their U.S. birth fosters an incomplete relationship with the black Caribbean community in the United States as it marks them as not quite Caribbean. The women's first-generation family members and friends frequently point this out. Specifically, they often classify the women as American when they fall short of black Caribbean standards. If the women do not "keep house" as expected by their mothers or grandmothers, if they exhibit behavior that is perceived as uncharacteristic of black Caribbean people (such as not showing appropriate respect to parents), or if they cannot prepare dishes in accordance with the standards of their islands, they are labeled American. Their American birth is used as rationale for the women's deviant attitudes and behaviors.

This classification is often partially done in jest and is perhaps more related to establishing, maintaining, and policing the boundaries between American and black Caribbean cultures than to the rejection of the second generation. Nevertheless, it helps to position these second-generation women as not fully Caribbean and create a discursive space for them to engage in selective cultural disassociations that foster flexible identities. By calling into question the participants' Caribbeanness, their in-group status, the "native" Caribbean people loosen the women's connections to the black Caribbean culture and thus foster a sense of liminality that enables these second-generation women to construct hybrid subjectivities. The women may not be *transnational citizens* (since they are physically located in the United States), but they are *transcultural* subjects who move between American and black Caribbean discourses to position themselves more advantageously in American society.

First, several of the women speak unapologetically about claiming an American (African American) identity in legal settings, such as when completing official documents and forms. In other words, some of the women choose to identify with the United States in official, bureaucratic contexts, where it may positively impact their access to economic and political resources. As Karrie says, "On paper, I like to be [called American]."

Additionally, while they embrace the Caribbean discourses of a good work ethic, education, and discipline, they actively rehearse negative ideas about black Caribbean norms and distance themselves from the Caribbean on these bases. More precisely, reflecting Western discourses, they talk about the Caribbean and black Caribbean people (those born and raised in the islands, to be exact) as chronically socially, politically, and economically underdeveloped. They take several measures to distance themselves from these negative conceptions that jeopardize their social and economic mobility.

For example, some of the women rehearse the prevailing conceptualization of black Caribbean sensibilities as incongruous with Western cultural and social spaces and incompatible with modern society. They distance themselves from this ideology by laying claim to American savoir faire.

This is predominantly manifested in the women's anxiety about exhibiting and divulging their black Caribbean culture in professional settings; they desire to hide the conspicuous signs of their heritage that connote unprofessionalism, namely, their accent and so-called informal behavioral tendencies. One respondent, Ronda, implies that black Caribbean culture must be unlearned in order to successfully participate in certain settings. She says: "In the business aspect . . . you know, because you are supposed to be professional and a certain way. I'm still learning how to be like that, really proper and upright." For her, a black Caribbean heritage does not translate very well in the American business culture and thus has to be modified and contained in professional settings.

Tamara shares her discomfort with her accent in her mainstream institution. She says,

> If someone asks me, I say I'm Jamaican . . . but just for purposes like in school and stuff like that, I talk regular or American. . . . I try so hard to hide [my accent]. Especially public speaking or speaking to my classmates, I try to hide just because I feel weird when it comes out when I'm trying to say a speech or something. . . . Like out of place, people are not going to understand. . . . Everybody's so focused on your accent instead of what you're trying to say. . . . I try to hide it. I try to practice and everything.

Tamara believes her accent draws attention to her "otherness" in ways that detract from the substance of her presentations, of her knowledge. This outward evidence of her cultural heritage undermines and possibly undoes her image as a serious student. In other words, her black Caribbeanness threatens to undercut her educational capital and her social mobility and status, so she distances herself from it in certain spaces. Brenda reinforces this idea when she says: "Once people hear an accent they automatically think less of you, that you're naive. The fact that I don't have an accent [is good for me]; they can identify more with you. You sound American."

Many participants also repeat contemporary discourses that mark the

English-speaking Caribbean and its predominantly black populations as infantile and simple, lacking exposure and unaccustomed to modern thought. In their identity narratives, the women construct black Caribbean culture as uncosmopolitan and unsophisticated and establish some distance from this reality by implying that their American socialization makes them different. For instance, Ronda believes that her Jamaican parents have an unprogressive response to issues of race and racism: "I . . . think it is because they are undereducated. Not saying they are dumb, because my mom is very smart but . . . [both] book wise and [exposure]. They have been in Jamaica for their whole lives. From what I know, I don't think Jamaica is diverse. I don't know anything much, but from what I see, I don't think it's that diverse." Ronda identifies as black Caribbean. However, her disassociation with the "nation" in this instance is evident by her use of the "othering" and distancing pronoun "they" in reference to her parents and by extension other people who spent most of their lives in Jamaica.

The response of another respondent, Tameika, implies a similar perception of black Caribbean people not born and/or raised in the United States. When asked if there are any aspects of her identity that she would characterize as American, she responds: "Open-mindedness. In America everything is exposed. It's not like Jamaica, where things are not as out there as in America . . . like affection in public, homosexual relationships." Another participant, Anita, highlights the conservative gender roles fostered and maintained in cultures of the Anglo-Caribbean. She says, "There is so much added pressure on Caribbean women to have to cook, you have to clean. . . . If you cannot cook, and you can't clean, you are *wutless* [worthless] . . . I don't subscribe to that . . . America allows more leeway in some of the areas." Her comment that she does not follow what she perceives as the conservative nature of gender roles in the Caribbean clearly separates her from the region and aligns her with perceived American gender egalitarianism.

These women criticize and distance themselves from the traditionalism and unprogressiveness that is often ascribed to black Caribbean people who live in the islands or who have migrated from there. The second-generation women, having been born in the global North, construct themselves as being of a different "world," the "first world" to be exact, and this fact makes them different from their island-born counterparts. Their American birth and socialization in the more "enlightened" space of the United States makes them more progressive than island-born and island-based black Caribbean people.

Other participants share discourses that pathologize the developing countries of the Caribbean as structurally flawed and perennially "third world," unfit to compete in the global economy. They construct the social structures and institutions of the region as peculiar, bizarre, and not at all like those of the United States, with which they are more familiar. In this way, the women deny being affiliated with the Caribbean and their underdeveloped social systems, which allows them to successfully distance themselves from the "third world-ness" of the Caribbean. One respondent, Veniece, reports that the inferior medical service in St. Vincent contributed to her uncle's death, cementing her distance from an island that she believes is incapable of caring for its people. She says that in the United States the doctors are more experienced and do everything in their power to keep you alive. Furthermore, people in St. Vincent will use homeopathic, traditional remedies, such as Vicks Vapor Rub and different types of teas, rather than advanced, modern medicine. So, while the women assert a predominantly black Caribbean identity, they concurrently reject what has been marked as the "third world" aspects of their heritage. By criticizing the Caribbean and foregrounding their preference for the institutions of the United States, the women align themselves with the reputation of progress ascribed to American society. This move establishes and constructs them as modern citizens of the developed world and neutralizes the "third world" designation given to other black Caribbean people with more direct ties to the islands.

In their statements, the Caribbean, its cultures, and the people who live or have lived there emerge as conservative, closed-minded and incompetent. In contrast, the United States is constructed as professional, modern, cultured, and open-minded. It is quite possible that the second-generation women acquired these ideas about the Caribbean through their interactions with American society. The perception of the Caribbean as chronically underdeveloped is embedded in U.S. ideology, policies, and practices. Specifically, the Caribbean is often conceptualized as indistinguishable islands of nothing but sand, sea, and sun, an image that essentializes and exoticizes the region and its peoples. Within this discourse, the Caribbean is constructed as exotic, connoting great physical beauty, but also unproductivity, traditionalism, and backwardness; it is a space that offers great vacation destinations but not much else. Its peoples are seen as warm and hardworking but incapable of innovativeness and avant-gardism. According to prevailing discourses, therefore, while able to reinvigorate tourists and visitors, the Caribbean does not have much to offer to modernity. This image persists in spite of narratives to the contrary, including the region's significant contributions to the global arts, athletics, critical thought, and religion.

The women have encountered these ideas about the Caribbean throughout their interactions with American society. As discussed earlier, they recount stories of being teased and ostracized in school because of their accents, and many were labeled as less intelligent by their teachers because of their black Caribbean heritage. They are also fully aware of the experiences of their relatives (particularly the women), who have often been dehumanized and marginalized within the classist, racist, and ethnocentric milieu of the United States largely because of their race and culture.

However, this conception of the Caribbean as pathologically undeveloped may also be cultivated by the first generation's own construction and projection of the Caribbean to subsequent generations. They disseminate narratives about the goodness of the Caribbean but also contradictorily discuss the problematic aspects of the islands: the economic hardships and high inflation, the "slackness" (informality) of business practices, the corrupt politicians, and the ineffective social systems. These characteristics often emerge from group discussions about the islands in which the first-generation immigrants, who remain deeply invested in their homelands, criticize their homelands, but many are frequently told to the second generation to emphasize their relatively "easy" life in the United States and to highlight the hardships that their predecessors endured. Whether attained directly or indirectly, these narratives necessarily inform how the second-generation women construct the Caribbean. Even if they have been to the islands, the second generation's experience and engagement with the Caribbean is mediated by the diasporic "nation," particularly the first generation. The latter's memories and histories shape the second generation's ideas about and experiences with the islands, leaving little room for counternarratives.

Overall, these identity narratives of the second generation reveal that the women simultaneously occupy two levels of awareness: they know how black Caribbean womanhood is constructed and performed (the values and mores, including the emphasis on education, discipline, and hard work), but they are also cognizant of neo-imperial discourses that "other" and marginalize their community, the ones that mark them as intellectually inferior and intransigent. The women deliberately engage both the positive and the negative discourses surrounding black Caribbean culture in the construction of their identities. They align with the community-constructed idea of black Caribbean womanhood even as they disassociate themselves from larger hegemonic discourses about black Caribbean culture that signify the "third world" and that are ultimately incongruous with their success in American society. Thus, while they embrace many norms and behaviors of their parents and the English-speaking Caribbean, particularly those that are celebrated in the American consciousness (such as respect, discipline, and being "laid back"), they distance themselves from the underdeveloped condition that has been ascribed to the region and its inhabitants.

By disassociating themselves from the black Caribbean culture on these grounds, the women indirectly align themselves with imperialistic consciousness; they reinforce neo-imperial global politics. Here their fluidity enables and is enabled by coloniality: they move between the black

Caribbean and American cultures because of ideas that are shaped by coloniality, and by doing this strategic shift, they reinforce neocolonialist ideas about the developed and the developing world. This strategic shift, their simultaneous embrace and rejection of black Caribbean and American ontologies, is indicative of their flexible identities. As demonstrated in chapter 4, this space of duality is furtive; it creates a borderland (Anzaldua 1987) that allows the women to challenge and resist hegemonic discourses and subsequently allows them to reimagine themselves.

Spectacle as Identity

In addition to constructing cultural liminality, some of the second-generation participants also present identity discourses that challenge the invisibility engendered by their location between black Caribbean and American cultures. Specifically, they discuss wanting to be conspicuous, to be noticed. Much of the discussion indicates that the women embrace the idea of being spectacles and being exoticized as a means to transcend this invisibility. For example, Karrie believes that a black Caribbean identity sets her apart from Americans, indicating her desire to create an "othered," exoticized presence in the United States. She says: "[Jamaicans] are different. When they are walking on the street, you know clearly they are not American. You know; it's just distinct. [They say], 'Okay she's not from here.' I like that. They're just very different, and I am all about being different, so I think that's why I identify with them more than [Americans]." Karrie, who also admits to identifying as American "on paper," simultaneously desires to remain perennially differentiated from Americans in the social sphere of the United States.

Other women, like Diane and Pamela, speak about using dress and accessories to be on exhibition and deliberately participate in their own exoticization. When asked about her ability to blend into mainstream American society, Diane boasts, "I don't fit in; I stand out. As soon as I go on the [subway], people are looking." Similarly, other respondents, such as Tony, Veniece, and Evelyn, take up current trends in American popular culture to inscribe difference on their bodies. They speak about employing piercings and other forms of self-expressive body art that make them stand out and that distance them from "regular" people.

Perhaps the most poignant comment in relation to standing out comes from a respondent, Akeyo, who sees her liminal position and the bicultural negotiations it entails as momentous and worthy of recognition, rather than pitiful. Reminiscent of the kinds of struggles and rewards that Gloria Anzaldua (1987) describes as being native to borderlands, Akeyo says: "I wanted to change the world, and I wanted to be remembered . . . as someone who was born in Jamaica but was raised in America and just understands the whole concept of two different lives . . . and how I expressed myself when I had those two different tasks put in front of me because it becomes one and that's what makes me who I am." This statement indicates that she believes she has an extraordinary life because of her cultural duality; her ability to negotiate a multifaceted identity makes her special and valuable in society.

This desire to be conspicuous and extraordinary is potentially indicative of the women's uneasiness with being in-between. They strategically move between the black Caribbean and American cultures in ways that are beneficial to them, but this flexible identity is neither comfortable nor unproblematic for them. Their statements imply their unwillingness to exist in the cultural limbo that tends to characterize the subjectivities of people who occupy multiple cultural spheres. People in this position often feel as if they do not belong, as if they are invisible. Tameika illustrates this when she says, "With Jamaicans, I know that I don't fit in because of my accent and everything about me says American. And to my American friends, I don't understand everything, but most things I do understand. When I speak to them, or when I'm explaining something to them, they might not understand, and that's when loneliness [may] impact me. . . . I feel like I have no place." Therefore, while their cultural hybridity fosters a place of power and subversion, it also engenders a form of psychic invisibility that the women have to contend with.

The women's desire and determination to stand out, to be different, also allow them to resist being tracked into the positions proscribed for them by coloniality. As black women with black Caribbean heritage residing in the United States, they are marked as unintelligent and expendable and are relatively invisible in the public sphere. By insisting on standing out, the women reject notions of their indistinctness (and passivity) in American society and project a level of self-directedness, ambition, and boldness that disrupts the metanarrative of marginalization that pervades black Caribbean women's involvement in U.S. society. Furthermore, the women's conspicuousness is enacted in ways that unapologetically draw attention to their persons, their bodies (through tattoos, clothing, and other outward symbols). These enactments are further indicators of the women's rejection of the rules of coloniality that dictate that their bodies are "monstrous." They are deliberately making themselves spectacles, but on their own terms.

Candidly, the discourses and performances of conspicuousness have a very individualistic, self-promotion tenure, as they are designed to empower and bring attention to the individual rather than to the struggles of the collective. I believe this characteristic reflects the contemporary so-called Facebook culture, which encourages routine publishing of personal postings and "selfies" that cultivate a sense of individualism and self-importance among its users. However, the women's attitude of self-importance reflects the confidence that is often reserved for women of privilege, the "beautiful" (that is, thin) white women of the global North, and thus, when enacted through their bodies, is at least partially transgressive in nature. This self-assurance and flexible identity facilitate a cultural maneuverability that allows the women to contest and circumvent the paths determined for them because of their race, nationality, and gender.

Diasporic Identity and Embodied Cultural Citizenship

The women's diasporic identities, their self-representation and construction in the United States, is directly influenced by their black Caribbean ethnicity; the cultural ideals, mores, and norms cultivated in the islands are undoubtedly a part of their subjectivities and inform how they perceive and position themselves in the United States. Their identity narratives are also shaped by the ideologies and experiences that structure their lives in New York City. Their responses to these challenges are absorbed into their self-definitions and intersect with the subjectivities cultivated through their association with the Caribbean. Black Caribbeanness for them is thus constructed by the environments of the United States and their homelands, the circumstances and conditions of where they are and the cultures in which they were raised.

Furthermore, given the women's active involvement in the shaping of their identities, their identity construction is a form a cultural citizenship, creating means to navigate and undermine the various challenges they encounter in the United States. The women's dominant identity narratives of the permanent foreigner and the flexible identity are the main ways in which they negotiate the intersections of race, gender, class, and Eurocentrism that they encounter in the various facets of their lives. These narratives reflect their struggles with downward mobility, micro-aggressions, and mediated stereotypes.

The narratives also shape and frame the women's interactions with beauty hegemonies, helping them to claim embodied cultural citizenship. In other words, the permanent foreigner and flexible identity narratives of the women inform the discursive and performative strategies that they mobilize to achieve positive body image and physical capital in spite of the social (and economic) disadvantages associated with deviant body aesthetics in the United States.

3 UNREQUITED ROMANCE
Black Caribbean Beauty Ideals and Discontent in the United States

Like other women of the African diaspora, black women of the English-speaking Caribbean put great emphasis on the voluptuous figure in their construction of black feminine beauty. However, we cannot assume that the "thick black woman" is monolithic across African diasporic cultures; this image is often interpreted and indigenized through the prism of culture and ethnicity so that there are variations in how it is manifested. Therefore, it is important to highlight the particular ways in which these women conceptualize and perform this ideal, especially when physically removed from the geographic space of the Caribbean. In this chapter, I explore the ways in which black Caribbean women in the United States imagine and enact the thick ideal. Through the personal narratives of black Caribbean women, I examine how the voluptuous body is articulated in the women's construction of beauty, how the women are socialized into this ideal, and the challenges they encounter in the United States because of their disparate construction of desirability.

The "Thick Black Woman," Caribbean Style

Both first- and second-generation women in the study conceptualize "thick" as the so-called Coca-Cola-bottle shape. As with the Coca-Cola glass bottle from which it derives its name, this silhouette is characterized by average-sized breasts, a small waist, a flat stomach, and, most importantly, generous (but proportionate) hips and buttocks. The women's preference for the voluptuous female body derives from their identification as black *and* Caribbean. As Tamara says, "I don't know if it's because I'm Jamaican or because I am black, but I just want curves."

The significance of racial identity in the women's construction of beauty is evident in their responses. The participants constantly refer to their preferred body as the "black shape" and the dominant American beauty ideal (thin, no curves) as the "white shape," the body image that white women pursue. Moreover, women in their community who do not have this body type are disparagingly referred to as "white" as a way to mark their difference, their deviation from the norm. As one respondent, Wendy, confesses: "I have nothing. . . . My mother's family all have [some] breast, large hips, and big butts. My father's family has large chest and small butts. . . . I have no chest or butt. I have to work with what I was born with. . . . [My family] call me 'white girl' because I have a straight shape. . . . It doesn't bother me. . . . I am just different."

The women in the study thus conceive of the thick body as intricately related to their racial identity; their equivalence of thickness with attractiveness is influenced by their self-identification as black subjects. For them, thinness is a characteristic of whiteness, while being thick is their "natural" inclination as black women. In this way, the women's comments highlight the belief that ideals of beauty vary based on race; they codify attractiveness along racial lines. This racialized discourse of beauty is reminiscent of colonial and contemporary ideas that claim there are genetically determined differences of bodies among races. Such notions reinforce a sociobiological construct in which one's body type, determined by race (skin color), dictates the abilities and intelligence one has and legitimizes racial discrimination.

Additionally, in this racialized discourse of the body, body shape (like skin color) becomes a defining feature of gendered racial identity.[1] More precisely, the voluptuous body becomes a representation and criterion of black femininity and thus fosters exclusionary practices; women who identify as black but do not achieve this aesthetic are labeled "white" or not "black" enough. Furthermore, the participants' statements reflect and reinforce the essentialization and reification of racial categories in the U.S. American racial discourse is excessively preoccupied with the relationship between black (specifically African American) and white Americans, to the exclusion of other racial groups in the nation. By discussing beauty standards along black and white lines, the women in the study rehearse and reinforce the black/white binary that characterizes racial politics in America.

The discussions by the women also suggest that racial differences in the construction of beauty and the idea of the curvaceous black woman are not limited to their community but are prolific and accepted in mainstream society as well. One respondent, Gina, explains the perception of her white peer, saying:

> If there were two girls standing side by side, both are size 12, one is white, one is black, she wouldn't see the black woman as overweight, but she'd see the white woman as overweight. . . . She's like, "I don't really think I've seen any person of color that's overweight to me," because in her eyes, she just sees that as normal. But then when she sees a white woman that's a little bigger, it's like, "Wow, that's sloppy," which I thought was interesting because you can see two women the exact same size, but just their color [makes a difference in how you perceive their size].

Another participant, Olivia, had a similar experience with her white friend: "[White people] expect [black women] to be a little bigger, thicker, so to them, it's not fat; that's how we're made up. . . . I have a friend of mine and [she] and I are pretty much the same size, and we would go working out together, go jogging, and I'm like, 'I have to try to lose my thighs, and my butt; I have to lose weight,' and she would say, 'You don't have to lose weight, you're perfect the way you are. I don't even know why you're working out with me.'" On the surface, it seems as if the comments and expectations of their white counterparts release them from the pressures of being thin. However, deeper reflection reveals that these comments are indicative of beauty discourses that place black women outside the dominant expectations of beauty. Because of their race, the participants are not expected to be thin (and beautiful); they are the bigger, less attractive version of their white counterparts.

Contemporary critics of the dominant American beauty discourses have long argued that the ultimate beauty in the Euro-American beauty regime is the thin, white body; thinness as well as whiteness are the central components and prerequisites of beauty, so black women (even thin ones) can never fully claim beauty in this system (Patton 2006; Shaw 2006; Craig 2002). In this way, beauty remains the exclusive domain of white women. As Andrea Shaw argues, the erasure of blackness is necessary in order to "render women viable entities by Western aesthetic standards" (2006, 1). Likewise, Susan Bordo implies that the popular perception of black women as immune to the reigning standards of slenderness serves to perpetuate "the racist notion that the art and glamour—the culture—of femininity belong to the white woman alone" (1993, 63). In this system, black women function as the "other" of white women (Hobson 2005): while white women are expected to embody beauty (thinness), black women are supposed to be their unattractive opposites whose lack reaffirms the beauty of white women.

The women conceive of the thick body not only as a marker of race but also as deriving from socialization or culture. They codify beauty along racial as well as *cultural* lines; they do not reify voluptuousness only because they are black women but because they are black women from the Caribbean. One respondent, Kenya, says, "Culturally [black people from the Caribbean] have a standard of what a woman should look like, but it is different from the American standard." Janet also says, "In the Caribbean, we all had Barbie dolls, but none of us wanted to be like Barbie. We didn't want to be that skinny."

The women speak extensively about the physical capital accrued to women who approximate the thick body, demonstrating the significance of this aesthetic in black Caribbean societies; they highlight the social acceptance, approval, and status that curvy women obtain in their communities, highlighting how the ideology of voluptuousness is cultivated and maintained through social-reward mechanisms. Evelyn articulates well the sense of fulfillment and belonging that women acquire when they achieve the voluptuous ideal. She says, "When I get big, I feel extra good about myself; I just feel like a woman. . . . I get that big confidence." Kenya discusses the social prestige associated with the voluptuous body in black Caribbean societies, including differential treatment in the public sphere. She says: "When I was skinny, the Americans would say, 'Oh you're so beautiful, you're so small.' However, my [black Caribbean] family would say, 'You need to eat, why aren't you eating?' . . . When I lived in St. Thomas, I was really skinny and I noticed the girls that got more attention in schools where the ones who were . . . thick or who had a heavy [big] behind." Karrie supports this claim by saying that, "I feel like the more body you have, the more [black Caribbean] men would pay more attention to you. . . . I think if you are not curvy, they are not looking in your direction in the Caribbean."

A Barbadian participant, Fiona, also highlights the approval she received when she gained the weight necessary to approximate the curvaceous ideal. She says, "When I went away to [college], I didn't put on the freshman fifteen; it was like the freshman thirty. And when I came back [home] for Christmas break, everybody was like, 'You filled out! You put on size!'" Similarly, another respondent, Amelia, shares how celebration of the thick body as well as negative cultural signification of thinness help to construct the boundaries of beauty in the English-speaking Caribbean: "When I was in Jamaica, you had to be thick; being thick was a sign of health. Being skinny was associated with poor health. I remember there was a girl who was the same age as me; she got all the attention. She had big boobs, big butt and everything."

The women also discuss the negative cultural meanings associated with thinness and the marginalization that comes from being too thin. They use strong imagery of diseased, emaciated bodies to convey their negative perception of the thin aesthetic. A Jamaican respondent, Marsha, says, "I don't look good skinny; if you see me skinny, I look very, very sick. I have . . . this nice big head, and everything else looks like . . . I'm getting over a bad flu, but when I full out, I look so good." Similarly, her sister, Sue, claims, "If I should decide to tone the way [American] society wants to see, I'd look like a crack head." A petite woman, Natalie, also shares:

> Recently I went down to ninety-seven pounds . . . and to know that I am going backwards to that . . . and you could see my collar bones and stuff like that. It was very traumatic for me. . . . I would complain all the time, and . . . look at myself and say, 'Oh my God, I don't look good,' and . . . I wouldn't get dressed in front of the mirror. . . . Now that I see that I am picking up back the weight, I think I'm comfortable now with myself. . . . I don't know if I haven't [dealt] with that part yet where I come to the acceptance it's okay to be skinny, but ninety-seven was just too much for me.

Brown Skin and "Good" Hair

As with other women in the African diaspora, the participants speak of beauty as also being associated with skin color or complexion.[2] Specifically, even though the women believe that it is not the only determinant of attractiveness, they agree that dark skin has less currency in their societies and thus dark-skinned women are considered less beautiful than their lighter-skinned counterparts.

For the dark-skinned participants, their skin color is a constant source of contention for them, one that began in their homelands and continues in the diaspora. One participant explains: "You had the *browning* and the *blackie*.[3] I had friends who were not more attractive, but they got the attention because I was not a *browning* . . . . After a while, I began to wish I was lighter with long hair. . . . I got teased; I was called *blackie, lippo* because of my thick lips. It made me self-conscious about my looks." Another respondent says: "In Jamaica, we don't have black and white; we don't have racism in that term, but I would have to work way harder than [a lighter-skinned girl] would. . . . My first job was at a bank and I was only one of three dark-skinned women." Similarly, another participant states, "In Jamaica the only issue I had was people saying, 'You are so beautiful . . . but yuh black.'" To emphasize that this colorism continues in contemporary times, one woman comments, "It still happens; the lighter-skinned person gets the job."

Because of the value placed on light skin, "bleaching" (the process of applying chemicals to the skin to make it lighter in color) is very prevalent in their communities, and that topic came up several times during the focus groups and interviews. All but one of the darker women in the study criticize and condemn this practice and refuse to go to such extremes to alter their complexion. Yet they are all cognizant of the fact that their darker skin tone deems them less attractive than their lighter counterparts.

Hair quality is also discussed extensively, as the women candidly express their struggles to achieve the ideal length and texture for their curls. In general, long, loosely coiled hair (referred to as "pretty" hair) is the ideal, which most black Caribbean women of African heritage do not have. Much of the women's discussion thus relates to their frustration with projects designed to force tightly curled, often thick hair into the acceptable texture. This includes using chemical processing, putting in straight or loosely curled hairpieces (weaves), and wearing wigs. Interestingly, while they denounce practices that alter the complexion, the women are less opposed to these hair projects. In fact, much like other works on the politics of hair in the African diaspora (see, for example, Banks 2000; Patton 2006; and the documentary *Good Hair* [2009]), I find that the women accept hair styling and dressing as a part of black culture and beauty ideals, developing a system of criteria for "good perms" and "good weaves" and seamlessly moving between processed hair, hair extensions, and wigs.

Evidently, skin color, hair type, and body size all figure prominently in the beauty ideals that the women present; a light-skinned woman with "pretty" or fine, long hair and a curvy figure is the ideal. However, while skin color and hair type are consistently discussed, body type emerges as the most significant feature of attractiveness. Based on the women's comments and my interactions within the community, light skin and "good hair" are preferred, but voluptuousness is a must-have, the non-negotiable, immutable part of beauty. Straight hair is desirable, but the lack of such hair type can be ameliorated (through hair relaxers, extensions, or embracing the natural look). A woman without this feature is thus not automatically marked as unattractive. Similarly, brown skin is preferred (as discussed in chapter 1), but dark-brown-skinned women are not completely excluded from being perceived as beautiful. Through such public events as the Miss Ebony contest in postcolonial Jamaica (Rowe 2009), postindependence English-speaking Caribbean societies aimed to celebrate blackness and raise the possibility of a desirable and respectable black woman. Perhaps owing to this deliberate movement, darker-skinned women, while perceived as less beautiful than their light-skinned counterparts, are not excluded from the domain of attractiveness.

Furthermore, because of the Anglophone Caribbean's complicated relationship with whiteness (which signifies slavery, colonialism, and unequal distribution of wealth in their societies), light skin, particularly the complexion that is close to white, has an ambiguous place in Caribbean society. True, women of this complexion have great physical capital and are routinely chosen as beauty queens and to be the faces of nations as well as companies (they are more likely to be hired in customer service, for example). However, they are also derided in working-class and low-income circles. They are called "reds," a derogatory term for people with their light color, and are seen as not black enough.

This ambivalence toward light skin in the Caribbean is evident when two light-skinned women in one of the focus groups share two different experiences: while the one from Jamaica recalls the privilege she gained growing up in the country because of her complexion, the one from Barbados recounts how she was ostracized because she was "too light." Therefore, while greater prestige is given to women with light skin in many arenas, dark-skinned women are not automatically rejected. In other words, the participants suggest that a woman who has a "good shape" but has neither light skin nor straight hair is still considered attractive. Therefore, the voluptuous body is the linchpin for the beauty constructed by the women, and it seems to be the part of their bodies that they emphasize. For this reason, this text focuses on body size and shape.

There are several important elements in the women's lives that influence their construction of beauty as voluptuousness, the primary ones being the black Caribbean community and popular culture.

Community and the Construction of Body Image

The women are surrounded by communities that help to construct, reproduce, and police their conception of beauty in the United States; these groups ensure that the women live up to the "thick black woman" beauty ideal promoted in the English-speaking Caribbean. These communities represent the black Caribbean "nation" in the diaspora; they play the role of "homeland" for these women, who are physically separated from their islands and the nexus of their cultures. It is this diasporic "nation" that does the practical work of writing discourses of embodied nationalism onto the bodies of black Caribbean women.

A significant part of the women's diasporic "nation" and an influential factor in their pursuit of the thick body is their families. Mothers, aunts, uncles, and even children help to police the women's bodies. These relatives carry out their cultural transmission through strict vigilance of and continuous commentary on the women's bodies, which are usually negative in nature. To ensure compliance and discourage deviation, relatives are quick to call attention to excessive weight gain and loss and weight accumulating in the "wrong" places (particularly around the stomach.) For example, Chela hypothesizes what her mother's response would be if she became thin. She says: "If I were to come home to my mom [looking skinny], she would probably say something is wrong. She would ask, 'Are you hungry?' I would say, 'No.' And she would say, 'No, you're hungry!' She is going to force some food on you!" Ronda also says: "My parents will remind me because they are blunt. [They say] things like, 'Why do you look like that?' or 'Why does your stomach look like that?' or 'You look like you've gained weight since you've been here' or 'Your belly is getting too big; you need to do something about that!'" Similarly, Sandra says, "In my family, you don't have to be really thick, just curves was the thing that was liked in my family, and also having a flat stomach was a really big, HUGE deal in my family, and I am often ridiculed for that. Jamaicans can exaggerate so a little stomach would be a huge [deal]."

For participants who were thin during childhood, their mothers and other family members compelled them to eat more, put them in lots of clothes to disguise skinniness, and later bought special clothing that would enhance breasts and other body parts they deemed lacking. One woman, Janet, speaks of her mother's efforts to "fatten her up": "My mom, she insists that you eat. . . . And I was very, as they say, *mahgah* [skinny] as a child, and my mother would put me in like two sleeves, to kinda pad up, and they make sure you clean your plate [eat all your food], cause this was normal, and having meat on your bones was the right thing, you know." Janet also shares her experience with being teased by her grandmother when she was younger and skinnier; this relative constantly asked her if she was thin because she "lived far from the kitchen." Another participant, Danique, says, "My mother, she [is] the one that sees it. She's like, 'You look skinny. . . . You need to eat something. You need vitamins; you need this.'"

The more voluptuous women whose bodies deviate from the "Coca-Cola bottle" ideal (such as those whose stomachs are deemed too big and whose overall size has passed the accepted ambiguous norm) also endure comments from their relatives. For Marsha, her confidence was completely shattered when at a family gathering a relative suggested that she was getting too big to be called "big-boned" and thus was no longer attractive. She relates: "I have an uncle . . . who used to tell me, 'Don't worry about it. You got big bone, you come from big bone.' So one day he said, 'You gonna still use that word *big-boned*?' So then that's when I know that I was getting too big and [that was his way of telling me]." Olivia's mother gives her advice about how to make her body better approximate the "Coca-Cola bottle" shape. She explains: "My mother says, 'You should get a good girdle to get rid of the gut, but if you wear it you're gonna lose;

you don't wanna lose the size. You wanna lose this [stomach] and not this [butt].' She is really looking at me trying to figure out how to make me look smaller [in my stomach] and leave [my butt] alone." Martha also says, "My mother sometimes says, 'Lawd, that belly don't look right.'"

As in many black Caribbean contexts, religious institutions also play a central role in ensuring that the women learn and pursue the voluptuous (not fat) ideal. Historically, churches have been instrumental in social reform as well as social control in the Caribbean; they play major roles in mobilizing people in the black Caribbean for activism against social injustices, but they have also been important entities in the maintenance of hegemonic systems.[4] In regard to the latter, churches are implicated in upholding the voluptuous ideology of the Caribbean in the diaspora. Specifically, they perpetuate surveillance of the participants' bodies and promote their bodily difference from white American women in the United States. For example, spiritual mothers are openly vigilant and critical of the women's size and shape. Olivia states: "I get [criticized] at home, but then at church, people are more critical. The people at our church, the older women. . . . This lady told me, 'Your hips cannot expand anymore; [you don't] have no [children] yet.'" Danique agrees, saying that one woman at church told her she had "too many dumplings" in her skirt. Clearly, family members and spiritual communities in the diaspora are important in passing on and policing cultural norms about black Caribbean beauty and helping the women to perpetuate the voluptuous ideology in the diaspora. The prominence of the diasporic "nation" in this process illustrates its role in transmitting cultural norms to generations more removed from the geographic and cultural space of the homelands.

Caribbean Popular Culture and Bodily Difference

The women's construction of beauty is also the product of socialization through black Caribbean popular culture, which they engaged in their homelands and continue to do in the diaspora. There are several media produced by and for black Caribbean immigrants living in New York City and the surrounding areas. This landscape is dominated by terrestrial radio (music) stations, web-based newspapers, and one television broadcast network, the Caribbean International Network (CIN). Furthermore, the women have access to media coming directly from the Caribbean through vehicles such as the Internet. The women turn to these media for information about the islands, specifically as related to news; they are popular destinations for up-to-date information about the social, political, and economic issues of the Caribbean.

These media also provide access to black Caribbean popular culture, particularly music such as dance-hall reggae and soca (calypso). The women routinely refer to and draw on the dominant discourses and images that are prominent in the music of the region to describe their ideas of beauty and attractiveness. Based on the women's statements as well as scholarly works, artifacts of popular culture, and personal observation, one sees that Caribbean popular culture generally esteems the thick body or women with a voluptuous figure. Round thighs and hips figure largely in this conception. However, the buttocks have a particularly special place in Caribbean popular culture, with fleshy posteriors being revered as a definitive sign of physical attractiveness and sexuality.

Lyrics of popular songs and their promotional videos are replete with imagery of thighs and hips and, most importantly, fleshy *batties* (buttocks). For instance, in one of the top party anthems of 2013 ("Pahty Tun Up" on the *Sweet Jamaica* album), internationally renowned dance-hall singer Mr. Vegas says,

> *Yuh bady look good, helty and fine*... [Your body looks good, healthy
>   and fine]
> *Bruk out mi gyal cause yuh physically fit*... [Revel and party,
>   my girl, because you are physically fit]
> *Natral bady gyal start work it* [Natural body girl start to
>   gyrate your hips].

The words *helty* (healthy), "physically fit," and *natral* (natural) are black Caribbean colloquialisms for the thick, voluptuous body that women are expected to maintain. Here Mr. Vegas speaks in celebratory terms about the *helty* body and implies the high social status that such a body engenders in parties and, by extension, the society. The song also encourages women with voluptuous bodies (the "physically fit" women) to *bruk out* (let loose), a notion that refers to untamed, unbridled behavior that is not a part of civil society as constructed by colonialist sensibilities. Mr. Vegas's call for women of this body type to participate in what is considered uncivil feminine behavior belies the link between thick bodies and uncivil behavior that is common in black Caribbean culture.

Indeed, there is a well-established ideological connection between big female bodies and excessive sexuality and lack of restraint in elite black Caribbean societies (Bakare-Yusuf 2006). There is a class dimension to this imagery as well, as this behavior is often associated with poor ("downtown") black women in Jamaica who exist on the margins of that society (Brown-Glaude 2011; Cooper 1995, 2004). In other words, the unruly thick black woman is a negative code for poor black women among the elites. However, by presenting the image of the thick body in positive and celebratory terms, Mr. Vegas's song inverts the unfavorable signification of that body.

Similarly, the popular soca song "Too Real" (2014) by Kerwin Du Bois (from the album *Soca 2014*) makes reference to the voluptuous ideal and its cultural and social significance. Du Bois sings,

> *Ah you gat di realest bumpah in dis town* [You have the best buttocks in this town]
> *Is the way you move it up and down*
> *An de size an de shape it's de way* [And the size and the shape, it's the way]
> *Dat yuh wine an yuh jiggle up yuh waist* [That you gyrate and jiggle your waist]
> *Dat bumpah is too real* [Your buttocks look so good]
> *It dangerous.*

Again, the lyrics illustrate discourses around the *batty* in the Caribbean and explicitly present the contradictions in how that image is perceived. The voluptuous body in this song is at once attractive and frightening, admired and feared, desirable but unruly. On one hand, having a voluptuous body is social capital, giving women prized places in society as indicated by being thought of as the "best in town." On the other hand, and reflective of the ideology of the elite class, that body signals a type of sexuality that is "dangerous" and uncontrollable. However, unlike the derision engendered by Eurocentric ideals, Du Bois's characterization of the large posterior as "dangerous" is a co-optation and inversion of Eurocentric ideologies meant to embolden rather than repress "fleshy" women. It speaks to a type of body and sexuality that cannot be fully controlled or "handled" by men in particular and society in general; it is one that engenders fear in keepers of the Eurocentric status quo. Such a body is thus a source of power because it is "dangerously" liberated from societal rules and constrains.

Mr. Vegas, Kervin Du Bois, and other artists in black Caribbean popular culture recuperate and reframe postcolonial ideas about the voluptuous black female body, rejecting the veneration of the slender European ideal and going against the norms of civility constructed by the ruling class; songs such as the ones discussed celebrate and encourage an "unruly voluptuosity" (Bakare-Yusuf 2006, 10). In this way, popular music of the Caribbean helps to create a beauty discourse that privileges and normalizes the thick black female body. As Carolyn Cooper notes in her study of the prominence of female sexuality and "slackness" in dance-hall lyrics: "The gender politics of the dancehall that is often dismissed by outsiders as simply misogynist can be read in a radically different way as a glorious celebration of full-bodied female sexuality, particularly the substantial structure of the Black working-class woman whose body image is rarely validated in the middle-class Jamaican media, where Eurocentric norms of delicate female face and figure are privileged. The recurring references in the DJs' lyrics to fleshy female body parts and oscillatory functions . . . signal the reclamation of active, adult female sexuality from the entrapping passivity of sexless Victorian virtue" (2004, 86). Similarly, Janell Hobson observes the celebration and empowerment of the voluptuous figure, particularly the *batty*, in black Caribbean culture: "Whether in working-class Jamaican dancehall settings or in carnival street scenes in Trinidad and the Caribbean Diaspora of Brooklyn, Toronto, or London, black female batties [derrières] are let loose and uninhibited in glorious celebrations of flesh and sexual energy. . . . Such movements of the batty, in the contexts of dancehall and carnival, invite a public discourse that challenges colonial constructs of 'decency' and 'white supremacy'" (2003, 101).

The dances designed for women in black Caribbean popular culture also celebrate the voluptuous body. For example, *wining* is a ubiquitous female dance style in the English-speaking Caribbean that entails circular movements and gyrations of the hips and buttocks. More than just a dance style, this move is meant to emphasize and put on display the curves of a woman's body. In fact, a woman's level of skill in this dance style is partially related to talent but also has a lot to do with body size; women with bigger hips and buttocks are deemed the better *bubblas* (women skilled at *wining*) and given high positions in the popular culture. The cultures' admiration and objectification of women who can *wine* can thus be seen as an extension of the veneration of women who have the thick body type and prominent buttocks. Relatedly, the prevalence of references to *wining* (and its variations) in black Caribbean popular culture is indicative of the centrality of the thick body in the construction of black Caribbean women's identity.

Wining is also a very sensual move that is used as a signifier of women's sexuality and ability to please their sexual partners. Therefore, better *bubblas*, often signified by women with voluptuous (though not fat) bodies, are seen as more sensual and feminine, more desirable and sexually empowered. *Wining*, and the requisite voluptuous body, is also associated with social empowerment. For instance, Richard Burton observes that it is "hardly coincidental that wining came to dominate the dance halls of Jamaica at precisely the time that the proportion of female graduates from the Mona campus of the University of the West Indies rose to an incredible 67 percent" (1997, 139). He goes on to say that *wining*, and the social forces it represents, challenges patriarchy and Eurocentric culture, making it one of the most important (and paradoxical) cultural development in the English-speaking Caribbean. Similarly, the increased presence of women (of all races and classes) and *wining* in carnival in Trinidad in the 1980s was seen (bemoaned, really) by many as an indication of the growing participation and assertiveness of women in economic and social arenas (Barnes 2000). While the positive connection between female power and *wining* is overstated and obscures less favorable responses to women's bodies in public spaces (I return to this point later), the privileging of such Caribbean dance styles for thick women does invite a public discussion of voluptuous bodies that celebrates and positively reframes the thick body in Caribbean societies and their diasporas.

Furthermore, women's fashion associated with these cultural forms is also designed to positively highlight and draw attention to the buttocks and thighs. The "sessions," "fetes," "dances," and carnivals of black Caribbean popular culture are occasions for women to be on display, to flaunt their bodies in clothing that best accentuates their *bumpahs* (buttocks) and thick thighs. As Bibi Bakare-Yusuf (2006) says, short pants outlining the genitals, micro hot pants (*batty ryedahs*), and figure-hugging short dresses are the most favored as they emphasize these important female assets. Granted, these types of clothing, especially when worn by black women "of shape," are condemned by civil society as vulgar. For example, to the ruling elites of Jamaica "the protruding belly, large dimpled buttocks and thighs squeezed into revealing batty riders mark . . . women as indecent, morally repugnant and unproductive elements within society" (Bakare-Yusuf 2006, 8). Natasha Barnes (2000) also points out how the shift from thematic costumes to spandex and string bikinis in Trinidadian carnival has created anxiety over the declining masquerading or "play" nature of the events and the dilution of its function in society. However, the presence of thick black bodies dressed in revealing clothing is also seen as an expression of black female empowerment. The flaunting of fleshy female body parts in revealing clothing, an image that is often excluded from and rarely endorsed in middle-class spaces, defies the ideals of civility and appropriate bodies that underline Caribbean elite societies. These popular clothing styles that foreground and expose the ample black female body are thus designed to reframe and celebrate voluptuousness.

These are examples of the rhetoric and performances that women in the study engage with in black Caribbean popular cultures, most of which foreground the "thick black woman" ideal. In many ways, these cultural forms reflect black Caribbean postcolonial politics that largely reject the civilizing processes of colonial powers as manifested in thinness and whiteness. For this reason, many view dance-hall and calypso music culture, with their emphasis on thick black female bodies and sexuality, as liberating (see, for example, the work on dance-hall culture by Carolyn Cooper). However, several scholars also criticize this music, for while it celebrates this body and its public display of unruliness, black Caribbean popular culture also simultaneously propagates ideologies that marginalize black Caribbean women. For instance, the lyrics, dances, and clothing styles reenact and embody male patriarchal stereotypes that depict women as sexually available. This construction of black women upholds males as voyeurs and creates an environment that fuels sexual harassment (Barnes 2000). In this sense then, as Barnes says, "women's visibility in Carnival [and by extension other spaces of popular culture in the English-speaking Caribbean] is more appropriately located as a terrain of struggle; it is a field of competing and contradictory desires where acts of libidinal self-assertion exist uneasily with the pleasures and real dangers of commodification and fetishism" (2000, 105). Moreover, though presented in a celebratory way, black Caribbean popular music's rehearsal of the link between black women's thick bodies and dangerous sexuality reinscribes colonialist notions that have negative implications for how real women are treated in societies within and outside the Caribbean.

Absent from the debate, however, are considerations of the beauty ideals disseminated by black Caribbean music and how they help to create and sustain the "romance" that black Caribbean women have with the voluptuous body. By consistently proffering the voluptuous body as the ideal, these forms of popular culture create and normalize a standard of voluptuousness for black Caribbean women (that is, they standardize the "thick" black female body). They propagate the ideology that black Caribbean women should be and are thick and *socialize* real women into accepting the "thick black woman" as the normal aesthetic of black Caribbean femininity. In other words, black Caribbean popular culture helps to shape the way that real black Caribbean women construct and perform beauty; it normalizes and reifies the dominant ideology of the voluptuous black woman and reminds women in the diaspora of what is expected of their bodies.

American Mainstream Media and the Voluptuous Ideal
The women also engage extensively with American mainstream media. Their tastes for these media are eclectic, varying greatly with each participant as well as among the women. Their media diet consists mostly of television series that include serious and comedic dramas, situation comedies, soap operas, and reality shows. Having lifestyles that are not always conducive to habitual and patterned television consumption, a lot of the participants record their favorite programs to watch them at their leisure. In most cases, they watch the shows alone or with whichever family members happen to be home at the time (often partners or children). If they have friends or colleagues who enjoy the same programs, the women discuss with them the latest plot twists or, in the case of some reality programs, the latest dismissals from the shows. Many women also routinely read magazines (both mainstream and those targeting the black community), and several frequently use the Internet and social media. In contrast, very few say they listen to American popular music because they prefer the music of their cultures.

The American media they are exposed to play a significant role in the women's socialization into the thick ideal. First, all the women proffer black women in the American media as examples of the ideal body type they espouse. The list of celebrities mentioned includes actresses Lisa

Raye and Tracy Ellis Ross, reality television star Nene Leakes, singers Nicki Minaj and Beyoncé, and first lady Michelle Obama. Interestingly, all the celebrities proffered by the women are American black women, and not black Caribbean or diasporic black women. Evidently, while these black Caribbean women may not identify culturally with black American female media personalities, they do recognize their common racial heritage and these celebrities' pursuit of the voluptuous ("black") body aesthetics. These stars stand out to the participants as women who uphold and propagate the voluptuous ideal of black women and present positive examples of the thick body.

Second, the women highlight that black women in the American media are presented as thick with bigger bodies while white women are thin. Brenda explains, "When you look at media, all the black women, huge hips, big butt, big breast. That's what they portray of a black woman in the media . . . and then the white girl is always skinny." Anita further illustrates this point: "If you watch a Justin Timberlake video, you have to be thin and trim; you have to be right. [On the other hand], that one Kanye song, talking about get your sit up right, you have to have a 'booty,' you have to have some hips, and you have to have some thighs." Chela concurs, saying, "The black singers always go for the [women] with the big butts and always put them in something tight to show the curves, but in the white [videos], they are kind of skinny and they don't really have that much."

Clearly, there are occurrences of slim or thin black women and characters (such as Olivia Pope of *Scandal*) and of white women who are more voluptuous. However, what is significant is how the women interpret what they see in the media. For them, the overall message from American media is that thinness is the domain of white women or women who want to be white, and the curvy body is for black women. Therefore, American popular culture is key in promoting, normalizing, and disseminating the thick black female body in American society and specifically among these participants. By repeatedly foregrounding voluptuous black female bodies in music videos and lyrics, television series, and magazines, American mainstream media reinforce to these women (as well as other audiences) the ideology that the normal and natural shape and size of the black female body is voluptuous and thick; they standardize the idea of racialized difference in beauty, cultivating a white/thin–black/curvy dichotomy.

Bittersweet Pursuit of Thick

The thick black female body is embedded in the racial and cultural identity of black Caribbean women in the United States and is reinforced by their diasporic communities, mainstream American media, and black Caribbean popular culture. The prevalence of this body type fosters the women's "romance" with the "thick black woman" ideology, the notion that black women are always voluptuous and thick. Nevertheless, the women's pursuit of the thick body is far from unproblematic. In fact, as discussed in the remainder of this chapter, their pursuit of voluptuousness creates many psychological, social, and professional challenges.

Body Image Trouble

The conception of the thick body in black Caribbean culture is more ambiguous than the music and women's comments lead us to believe. Not being grounded in measurable clothing size, the actual dimensions of that body are relatively imprecise for the women who have to tread the very fine line between being desirably thick and unattractively fat. Even though the thin black female body is marginalized, the "fat" body is not acceptable. The women do not view plump, round bodies that do not approximate the "Coca Cola bottle" shape as desirable; they do not want to be *wagga wagga*, as Ronda explains: "Jamaicans have this phrase that they don't want you to become 'big and *wagga-wagga*' [large in body size, out of shape, and lacking bodily proportion]. And that's the phrase that I grew up with from my parents. I feel like that whole phrase wraps up body image for the Jamaican culture. Just don't become too fat where your body and your rolls [stomach] are all over the place because then that's unacceptable."

In sum, the thick body is an undefined one, and the women struggle to maintain the delicate balance between being too skinny and too big. This negotiation promotes the women's continuous obsession with and vigilance of their bodies, resulting in frustration, neurosis, low self-esteem, and ultimately lack of confidence in their ability to participate in the public sphere. In fact, it is the women's endorsement of this nebulous not-too-big-not-too-small aesthetic that engenders many of their physical insecurities and, subsequently, fuels constant body-improvement projects. The bigger women in the study speak about their desire to lose the weight that has accumulated in the "wrong" areas and make their bodies better approximate this curvaceous image; they use a variety of methods to gain bigger or smaller breasts, smaller stomachs and larger buttocks, as illustrated by the following statements:

KENYA: Now I have a [stomach], and I am depressed. I wonder how do I get rid of it!

DANIQUE: I definitely want to lose my [stomach], and keep my [larger] butt, because I never had a butt before.

GINA: I have done so many things [to get this shape]. I have done the Beyoncé diet with the cayenne pepper.[5] . . . I did the clear wrap with the Saran wrap, the green tea . . .

SUE: I would love more booty [buttocks], less boobs, but I've learnt, since I can't afford plastic surgery right now, I minimize [my boobs]; I just gotta work on the butt. Overall my pet peeve with my body is the [stomach]; I need to work on that. Everything else I truly like.

The thinner women are equally consumed with the ambiguous "Coca-Cola bottle" shape and also engage in dieting behaviors designed to avoid degeneration into the undesirable "white" skinny body type, that is, the hipless, buttless thin silhouette of mainstream America. One such participant, Shaunie, confesses, "I used to be very, very slim, and I didn't get a positive response [from family and friends]. I started to eat in order to gain weight." She does not know how big she needs to get, but based on continued unfavorable responses to her body, she knows she has not yet attained it. In other words, her ideal size is achieved when she receives social rewards from the black Caribbean community. The women's anxiety about maintaining the ideal size and voluptuous shape is captured perfectly in Danique's account of the fluctuation of her weight:

> I was maybe a size 4 or 2; it wasn't cute at all, at all. . . . [Then] I was like a size 8 until I got to fifteen, sixteen I started to go down. . . . In a short period of time I lost a lot of weight; and I was nice. . . . When I started to work I started to put on back normal weight, and I really did look good, but I was gaining weight now. Now I am like a size 8; I am gaining weight now and I am freaking out because I am getting fat.

These statements reveal the problematic nature of the thick ideology. While the voluptuous figure is a part of the women's cultural and racial identity and they pursue it at great lengths, it has an ambivalent place in their consciousness. They embrace the thick body type, but in spite of its endorsement of larger, seemingly healthier aesthetics, it is a patriarchal normalizing mechanism that engenders self-contempt in the women and undermines their body image. This insecurity that it fosters is no small matter, as it can also undermine the women's confidence in pursuing social and economic mobility. It can fuel an inferiority complex that influences the assurance necessary to succeed in a competitive world. Therefore, perpetuation of the "thick black woman" ideology upholds patriarchal systems that promote black Caribbean women's obsession with their bodies.

Diasporic communities and black Caribbean popular culture function as the custodians of the "thick black woman" ideology and are therefore implicated in the body-image issues that the women face. Granted, their promotion and celebration of a bigger (though admittedly, not fat) aesthetic challenge the existing discourses that value only thin bodies. However, the reification of the "thick black woman" also creates a normative standard that the women have to live up to, which has negative implications for their well-being. First, they both promote complicity with a beauty standard that disempowers the women. The vigilance with which the diasporic "nation" watches over the women's bodies and the preponderance of discourses from Caribbean music that promote the thick body prevent the women from deviating too far from the expected norm. In doing so, the activities of the diasporic communities and their popular culture require the women to align with an essentialized image of black Caribbean beauty and constrain the agency that they have to pursue other ideals. In other words, these socializing entities encourage the women to perpetuate a beauty ideal that may not be in their best interests.

Second, while intended to mold young girls into women who will be admired and accepted in black Caribbean societies, the comments of their biological and surrogate mothers and relatives significantly contribute to the women's neurosis, self-consciousness, and obsession with body size and shape that many are still trying to overcome. The effects of the objectification that the women experience because of this surveillance and scrutiny are manifested not only in their anxieties and frustrations about their bodies but also in their emotional states. Several of the respondents are candid about the level of distress they experience because of the ambiguous policing. Some of the women admit that it is only in recent years that they have learned to ignore their families (because they continue to "harass" them) and accept their body size and shape.

Two accounts are particularly agonizing. Karrie shares an emotional moment when she finally confronted her mother and aunt about their relentless comments on her body. She is a petite woman, but she had begun to gain weight in the "wrong" areas, and these two relatives would constantly highlight her deviation with displeasure and express disapproval at what and how much she ate. She says: "One day, I just couldn't take it. [I said to them], 'Don't talk to me like that. . . . Why would you say something like that? You don't know if I'm going through anything. . . . Don't sit there and judge me, and tell me that I'm big, and I look bad. . . . That's not nice.'" By linking her body size to her mental health, Karrie challenges her mother's and aunt's separation of body and mind and calls for a more holistic (less patriarchal) way of engaging with issues of the female body. She was hurt by her relatives' comments about her weight, as well as by what she perceived as their undue focus on her physical self and neglect of other aspects of her being; in other words, she was hurt by their objectification (and dehumanization) of her, the implication that her body is the most important part of her being.

Anita also highlights the neurosis engendered by her family's objectification of her body. Throughout her life she has received multiple and contradictory comments about her body, which have led to her obsessive monitoring and sculpting. She says: "I was very skinny. I was called anorexic, and at my house, they were complaining that I didn't finish my food. They [her family] claiming I am not eating enough, and then when I started putting on weight, I went home winter break, and [that Christmas], every minute [someone would ask], 'Anita you put on weight?' . . . You can see my weight gain in my face, so now I have to go lose weight." The frustration Anita felt is replicated in the focus group as the other five women try to make sense of the myriad critiques she has received with repeated questions of, "What do they want from you?" The discussion ends in exacerbation, however, as Anita is not able to decipher and articulate what her family required of her body. She just knows she has to be in the middle in order to be accepted as an attractive black Caribbean woman.

Furthermore, the musical forms of the Caribbean also create angst for the women as they foster discourses of beauty that create self-dislike in women who do not approximate this body type. Indeed, several of the women in the study share the dissatisfaction they feel with their too-small buttocks after listening to or watching black Caribbean media that promote this ideal. Therefore, while black Caribbean popular music provides an alternative environment that reframes the thick figure as capital (undermining the primacy and normalization of the thin body and Eurocentrism), it also cultivates discontent with bodies that do not fit the curvy ideal.

Thick Bodies and Negative Physical Capital
In addition to damaging personal and psychological consequences (as discussed earlier), black Caribbean women's "romance" with the voluptuous

ideal also creates challenges for them in the larger American society. They are surrounded by communities and popular culture that encourage and celebrate the thick ideal, but they have to engage with an American society that reifies thinness (and whiteness) as ideal femininity. This creates negative physical capital for them.

The women are very forthcoming about how their race and body size and shape contribute to their social ostracism in the United States. One respondent, Lilli, says, "In certain environments [in the United States] I feel fine; in others, I feel like people are judging and looking. I was in an environment that was predominantly white women and they were thinner than I am. I felt that they didn't want to look like me because they believe I am too big." Analogously, using the male gaze as the barometer for social acceptance and status, Sue compares her experience of being a thick-figured woman living in Jamaica and the United States and the diminished social status that accompanies the latter: "Men in Jamaica will make you appreciate your [big] body just a little bit more than the men here. You could have like six rolls here or whatever, if you put on some [shorts, they will say], 'Baby! Psst, psst! You looking sexy.' Here in New York, they just look at you, 'Oh lord, look at her. She need a diet . . . All the rolls. La'ad, she big!'" Marsha also says, "I am heavy with a stomach and nappy hair. If I and a slim girl was walking down the street [in the United States] and there is a man on the corner, no matter how nutty she is, he would choose her over me. He would not see me. . . . It's still kind of interesting like for me if I walk down the street and get a comment from a particular guy. In the back of my mind I'm always going, 'Is that person talking to me?' because I'm not a size 2."

Interestingly, black Caribbean men in the diaspora also contribute to the women's uneasiness with their bodies in the United States. Several of the participants discuss what they see as the change in preferences that men undergo once they migrate. One participant, Oma, says: "When some men migrate they change; they no longer want the voluptuous women; they want skinny with long hair and brown skin. Most Jamaican men are dating Spanish women [when they come to the United States]." Similarly,

Sue explains: "When they come here, they get culturalized, and you know the skinny girl, long hair, the nails and stuff; you have to have the flare. But then when they back home and you [with a thick body] there, they all over you." The comments illustrate the importance of the male gaze in the women's comfort with pursuing a more curvaceous body, supporting literature on perceptions of beauty that suggest that being desirable to men is a strong determinant of the internalization and replication of beauty norms (Bordo 1993). Their comments are also criticisms of black Caribbean men, who the women believe change based on cultural contexts and apparently abandon their culture once they arrive in the United States in efforts to align with dominant U.S. ideologies. More significantly, this perceived change in black Caribbean men contributes to the frustration the women feel with maintaining the thick ideal in their new homes. Not only do they feel out of place in mainstream American society, but their bodies are now considered undesirable by men of their own culture.

The women's exclusion and rejection are also experienced in relation to clothing, illustrating how the beauty hegemony of thinness operates through the fashion industry. The women discuss the difficulty they have finding clothing that suits their bodies, and the feelings of abnormality, unattractiveness, and otherness this cultivates in them. Gina states that "It's hard to find clothes that fit. Now I feel like I have to lose weight, because I want to fit in." Analogously, Kenya poignantly highlights the way that mainstream clothes position her body as abnormal. She says, in exasperation: "The way the clothes are designed, even if you purchase your size, the pants will fit snugger in the thigh area for women with thick thighs. The pants aren't necessarily made to accommodate this body type. Who are they using as templates to design these clothes? I don't understand the proportions! It is not made for my body type." Olivia concurs with Kenya, saying, "[Black Caribbean people] look at me and they're like, 'Why you complaining; you're fine . . .' Yeah, but when I put my clothes on, I don't feel comfortable in my clothes." Ronda also generally feels "okay" about her body but is frustrated with what is offered in stores. She says, "Tell you the truth, sometimes when [clothes] are on sale . . . they only have the small sizes!" Sue, one of the bigger women, also shares her apprehension about wearing certain kinds of clothing, given her voluptuous figure. She says: "Somebody see me coming, I know exactly what they thinking: did she have mirrors in the house? Did she get dressed in the dark?" Marsha, another full-figured woman, talks about being comfortable with herself, but being frustrated with clothing choices: "I [can't] buy anything anymore. Now I start, instead of wearing the pants, I buy elastic. Those elastic can expand. . . . At times I go in the store and I can't find anything that I really, really want."

The fashion industry is thus instrumental in codifying their voluptuous bodies as strange and malformed. By predominantly producing and selling clothing that fits and compliments the slender, hipless body, the mainstream fashion industry highlights and perpetuates the unwillingness of American society to acknowledge and venerate women of their body size and shape. Furthermore, by refusing to produce clothing that suit and fit their curvy bodies, designers force the women to wear ill-fitting clothing or retreat to less appealing styles, thus reinforcing their perceived abnormality and marginalizing them in the social sphere.

By limiting their clothing choices, the fashion industry also constrains the women's professional movements. The women who work in white-collar, white spaces (corporate America) candidly discuss the difficulty they face in finding professional clothing that suits and compliments their body shape and size and talk about the subsequent self-consciousness they feel about their bodies in their offices. As Fiona relates, "I try to get rid of my butt because I don't fit into my clothes. I work in corporate America so I buy the clothes that all the white people make, Calvin Klein, Tahari, and I don't fit into [their pants] for anything. . . . [My butt] is the one thing that does not fit into anything. . . . The clothes don't fit with my body type; my body doesn't fit with the clothes, so I'm just trying to assimilate to be able to fit into my clothes to fit into [corporate America]." With scant availability of professional-style clothing for women of their body type, the fashion industry proscribes the spaces that these women can enter, which may have significant implications for their economic mobility.

In addition to the politics of clothing, the women also have to contend with social commentary that persistently draws attention to the inappropriateness of their bodies in professional spaces, and thus their unsuitability for this sphere. The women are candid about the judgmental comments they receive from coworkers about their "big" hips and thighs and the differential attention they receive when wearing the same type of clothing as their white female colleagues. The following exchange between Kenya and Martha is emblematic of the general feeling among the women:

KENYA: I was told at work that my pants were tight, but they weren't; I just happen to have bigger thighs.

MARTHA: I have that same problem. I had a similar situation where I was told my pants are too tight. I commented that if you put a Caucasian of similar size in the same pants the fit would be completely different. I tried to make light of the situation by saying, "Don't blame me because I have a really good figure." I tried to not make it an issue.

The dearth of professional clothing that suits their silhouette and the unfavorable reactions to their bodies in professional spaces underscore the systemic marginalization and exclusion of these women in professional spaces. Not having business attire made for their bodies and having to routinely suffer comments about the impropriety of their bodies in office spaces are situations that explicitly classify these women as unsuited for the professional, modern world. In this way, then, the women's race, nationality, and body size are seen as markers of not only unattractiveness but also unprofessionalism and signify their incapacity to contribute much value to that setting. In other words, their thick bodies are deemed out of place, spectacles, in these contexts. Maintaining the black Caribbean standards for body size and shape therefore exacerbates their simultaneous hypervisibility and erasure in mainstream organizations. Their thick black bodies stand out in their mostly white professional spaces, and those bodies are used to "silence" them and exclude them from the intellectual life of this sphere. This thick body ideal thus gives fuel to existing discourses that foreground their bodies and ignore their intellectual worth and the contributions they can make to these organizations. In this way, American mainstream society uses the discourse of the "thick black woman" to marginalize them in the most lucrative spaces of their societies. This conception is replicated and synergized across different fields, from the fashion industry to offices, and I believe it propels a global neo-imperial project that creates and promotes the women's unequal access to resources and their subjugation in economic and social arenas.

This brings me back to the idea of color-blind racism. Assigning voluptuous bodies to black women and then marginalizing them for it reinforces the ideology of color blindness. I argue that the "thick black woman" ideology—the idea that all black women are voluptuous—is another frame that helps to underscore racial inequality without overtly using race. In other words, while race is central to discrimination against black women in American society, foregrounding their size and shape allows dominant society to explain their marginalization as a result of the inappropriateness (grotesquerie) of their bodies; it provides a way to position black women as abnormal without using the color of their skin. In this "postracial" moment in the United States, it is politically incorrect to openly acknowledge black women's race and exclude them on that basis. The shape and size of their bodies, on the other hand, can be openly examined, discussed, and critiqued and used to dismiss them. Furthermore, since their body aesthetic is a cultural signifier and referent for their race, discussing their bodies is an indirect, less overt discussion of race, one that circumvents skin color. In this way, black women can continue to be marginalized, but under the guise of body politics (disparate care, presentation, and regulation of the body) that do not align with those of the professional world of the United States.

In this sense, then, this signifier of their cultural identity intensifies black Caribbean women's outsider positions in the United States and further constrains their participation in certain spheres. Black Caribbean women's cultural and racial subjectivity actually helps to cultivate a body type that further puts them at a disadvantage in their new home; by practicing and upholding black Caribbean beauty ideologies, the women perpetuate a system of beauty that challenges the reification of thinness in the global North, but that also deepens their marginalization in the United States.

The preceding statements expressing their social, sartorial, and professional marginalization reveal that the women's issue with the hegemony of thinness that operates in U.S. society is not that it pressures them to be thin per se. Rather, their anxieties derive from being positioned as unequal to the (white) thin body in this regime, having their racialized and cultural bodies marked as monstrous. In other words, within the thin beauty hegemony of the United States, these women are not necessarily negotiating pressures to be thin (to pursue a thin ideal), but rather they are struggling with the negative physical capital that they encounter because of their voluptuous bodies.

The women feel that the negative physical capital created by their curvaceous bodies further complicates their positions as immigrants in the United States. Their place outside the thin ideal presents yet another obstacle to their prosperity in the United States as it unfavorably affects their ability to fully succeed as immigrants. I argue that this has social as well as economic implications. As immigrants, many of whom bear the responsibility for the economic support of their families in the United States as well as the Caribbean, their diasporic activities are at least partially centered on economic success in the United States, that is, their ability to earn money. In fact, as discussed in chapter 2, black Caribbean women generally embrace the idea of industriousness, hard work, and productivity—having a job and financial stability—as a significant aspect of black Caribbean women's diasporic identity. Not having access to some parts of the American society and economy (because of their race, their accents, their culture, as well as their body type) hinders their participation in the most lucrative parts of U.S. society, and, I argue, negatively affects their ability to achieve financial stability and security. This reinforces Chris Shilling's (1991) assertion that physical capital (or the lack thereof) contributes to reduced economic opportunities and social inequalities.

So, while black women such as these black Caribbean respondents may be relatively unreceptive to pressures to be thin, they are significantly impacted by the corollaries of the thin ideology; they have to exist in a beauty hegemony that devalues and punishes their unthin bodies and undermines their positions in the United States. Therefore, the beauty regime of thinness not only operates "*despite* celebratory politics [of thickness], but indeed [is] *reproduced and affirmed by it*" (Murray 2005, 162, emphasis in original).

American Media and Double Consciousness

In addition to negative physical capital, black Caribbean women also struggle against American mediated discourses that present unfavorable counternarratives about the voluptuous body. Specifically, in spite of their own culturally and racially driven desire to pursue voluptuousness, American mainstream media generate negative affect toward their bodies by locating their thick bodies outside the realm of normal. Once again, the women's responses show that they are not frustrated with the thin ideology propagated through media because it compels them to be thin. Rather, they have anxieties because mediated discourses set up thick black women for failure.

As discussed earlier, dominant American mediated images and discourses normalize the voluptuous body for black women and reinforce for the respondents that as black women, they should be big. However, the women also recognize that these media simultaneously reify the thin white body as the desirable aesthetic. They point out that black women of their body type (curvy or voluptuous) with dark skin rarely show up in American mainstream media. They often appear in niche, "black" media and are rarely seen in mainstream television, movies, and magazines. When they are present, they are depicted as different or separate from the thin, white norm. Their race and body shape (which are usually accompanied by "urban black" vernacular and attitudes) frequently provide comic relief, and they often play the roles of the sassy, irreverent, abrasive characters who are included to underscore the main (white) characters' postracial sensibilities and existence outside "normal" society. In other words, whiteness and thinness are privileged as the standard, while black-ness and thick bodies are represented as spectacles.

Additionally, black women in mainstream American media routinely have their physical and cultural blackness "diluted" or erased and their bodies slimmed down. Beyoncé comes up a lot in this regard during the in-terviews and focus groups. Some women identify her as a good example of the ideal black figure: flat stomach, thick legs, prominent buttocks. Often, though, this megastar is used to illustrate how the media undermine and marginalize black women's bodies. Specifically, the women discuss how the media "whiten" Knowles, literally and symbolically. They highlight the lightening of her skin through Photoshop so that she appears lighter over the years. They also highlight how media discourses position her as French or mixed race but never black, thus undermining her "blackness." Furthermore, the women comment that her media representations (in magazines and commercials) are significantly smaller than her real-life size. The media practices that the women describe send a very distinct message: women of their race and body size are undesirable; beauty is not and cannot be thick and black, especially when dark-skinned.

Through these mainstream American mediated discourses, the women are constantly given the message that as black women, it is normal for them to be thick, and further, they are *supposed to* be thick. However, it is the thin body (the exclusive domain of white women in mediated discourses) that is paraded across the media as beautiful, successful, and competent, while voluptuous black women are comparatively constructed as grotesque and out of place in society. American mainstream media thus help to construct, uphold, and propagate the expectation of the "thick black woman" ideology but simultaneously promote the marginalization of women who pursue or embody this ideal. In this way, the thin ideology in media is not simply about promoting thin bodies but is also about perpetuating a thin hegemony that creates an environment of privilege for white thin bodies, on one hand, and marginalization for thick black bodies, on the other.

This American beauty hegemony promoted in the media is problematic for the women. First, it normalizes their subjugation in U.S. society; by systemically marginalizing voluptuous black women, media cultivate the idea that it is normal for black women with bigger bodies such as theirs to be relegated to or excluded from certain spaces in real life. Second, it contributes to the dissonance that the women experience about their bodies. More precisely, and as mentioned earlier, the thin regime promoted by media simultaneously standardizes the "thick black woman" ideology and ostracizes black women for it. This discourse creates conflict for the women who are encouraged to embrace voluptuousness as a part of their cultural and racial identity but who are also told that this ideal is inferior. This situation makes it difficult for the women to be at ease with their bodies in the United States; they struggle with what their bigger bodies signify in the beauty hegemony of the United States. Kenya says: "It is hard when you have to deal with it day in and day out. When you are at work, when you go shopping, every time you turn on the television. We might believe that it doesn't affect us; however, subconsciously it does." Kenya indicates that media help to construct a totalizing environment, a pervasive system in which the curvy black female body is condemned and dehumanized.

Ronda also poignantly discusses her struggle: "When I look at myself in the mirror, based on my Jamaican culture that's in me, it's like okay, you have meat that's on you and that's okay because some guys are going to like that, and you know, you don't want to be bony. [sighs] But another part of me sees that girl on the American magazine with her long straight hair or nice curly hair and just everything looking all perfect on her. No pimples, all makeup all over her, skinny . . . and it's kind of like, 'Maybe I need to be like that.'" So media, with their constant presentation of the thin hegemony, make her view her body as abnormal and "wrong." In spite of the social acceptance and mobility that the thick body engenders in black Caribbean culture, when she looks at her body through the prism of American mainstream media, she realizes that it is not a part of the norm and is invisible; she is invisible. Ronda is thus aware that her maintenance of a thick body creates the situation in which she is marginalized, absent from American media and society. Sue shares a similar sentiment. She says: "Television doesn't make it easy to be big. That show, *Biggest Losers*, everybody that comes on is humongous, and then in . . . two months, four months they go down. I'm like, 'Okay. Should I call them up, and get on the TV?' It's a free way of losing the weight." In other words, television shows, particularly those that explicitly demonize big female bodies of any race and present thinness as the only path to redemption, threaten her self-confidence and the relatively positive manner in which she perceives her body.

In this sense, then, American mainstream media construct a cosmetic gaze for the women. According to Bernadettte Wegenstein, the cosmetic gaze is one in which "the act of looking at bodies and those of others is informed by the techniques, expectations, and strategies of bodily modification. It is a moralizing gaze—a way of looking at bodies as awaiting a physical and spiritual improvement" (2012, 2). Said differently, the cosmetic gaze is a way of viewing one's body as always lacking and in need of transformation. This way of seeing dates back to Plato's concept of *kalokagatheia*, which identifies a direct relationship between outward appearance and inner essence or beauty, the belief that one's physical appearance is an indication of the goodness of one's morals. Over the years, several groups have been tasked with being (or have taken it upon themselves to be) the authoritative gaze that determines the "better beautiful" (Wegenstein 2012, 111), including physiognomists and racist theorists. In twenty-first-century Western culture, "this 'better beautiful' version of the self has been identified as a commodity by aesthetic surgeons and software engineers who develop 'beautification machines' of the 'ideal you,' and they are proliferated at the speed of light through our current media culture" (111).

Media, particularly makeover shows, allow audiences to internalize the cosmetic gaze by helping them to envision the virtual, mediated bodies of reality stars as their own bodies and highlighting the personal and economic capital that can be gained from changing their bodies into their better selves. These media create an environment filled with makeover bodies that tell audiences how they should look and produce a desire for their own makeovers. This conveyance of the gaze facilitated by the media makes it difficult to be happy with oneself (Wegenstein 2012); once you begin to see yourself through the made-over bodies of the augmented reality of media, it is difficult to accept your current body as normal. The women's comments imply that they are caught in a racialized version of this cosmetic gaze; as black women who have or desire bigger body aesthetics, they interpret their bodies through the mostly white mainstream media as always in need of change, of not being racially or aesthetically good enough.

Transmission of the cosmetic gaze by American mainstream media also plays a significant role in the creation of a form of double consciousness. According to W. E. B. Du Bois, black people in America are "gifted with second-sight . . . a sense of always looking at one's self through the eyes of others, of measuring one's soul by the tape of a world that looks on in amused contempt and pity" (1903, 9). This double consciousness creates "contradictions of double aims . . . that seek to satisfy two unreconciled ideals" (Du Bois 1903, 2). It is characterized by being pulled or pressured by contradictory exigencies; black people hold the desire to maintain, nurture, and speak to the ideas, cultures, and consciousness of their people but are simultaneously cognizant of the need to seek acceptance, inclusion, and economic capital in the white world that disparages, ridicules, and tries to stamp out blackness.

American mainstream media cultivate a similar "second-sight" for black Caribbean women living in the United States. These women value the voluptuous body type, but they exist in a diasporic space that nurtures and upholds colonialist discourses that exoticize, debase, and ostracize that body. The mainstream media, which present thinness as the ultimate success and achievement, as the only path to happiness and fulfillment, play a significant role in normalizing, projecting, and disseminating these discourses throughout society, including in black Caribbean communities. They also cultivate the idea that thick black female bodies are natural but grotesque and valued only for reproduction and menial labor. The display of these ideologies in media forces voluptuous black women to see themselves through the eyes of Eurocentric society and interpret their bodies according to the scripts outlined by dominant American body politics. They make the women view their bodies through the prism of dominant American society and persuade them to accept the hegemonic readings of their bodies as natural for them but ugly, out of place, and irrevocably in need of change.

For these participants, then, mainstream American media serve to undermine black Caribbean peoples' positive reframing of the "thick black woman" image, compelling the women to accept the voluptuous body as normal for them but as grotesque and inferior to the thin body. Therefore, the women's distress does not necessarily come from their inabilities to attain thin bodies, but rather they experience angst because of their "second-sight," their awareness (informed by the cosmetic gaze constructed by the media) of the contempt, pity, and condescension with which their bodies are perceived in white American society. In other words, the construction of beauty in American mainstream media fosters their double consciousness and lowered body image.

4 TRANSGRESSIVE DISCOURSES
Negotiating the Thin Hegemony and Negative Physical Capital

All the women in the study clearly experience multiple layers of "embodied crisis." They pursue a bigger body size but struggle with achieving and maintaining that ideal, and while they reject the thin-body aesthetic, the women still have to exist and function in a society where their non-thin bodies exacerbate their marginalization and curtail their participation in mainstream spaces. Existing outside of the beauty discourses in the United States has significant implications for their ability to fully participate in their diasporic space. They also grapple with the double consciousness fostered by mainstream American media. Therefore, in addition to dealing with the complexities and contradictions of living within the voluptuous regime of black Caribbean culture, the women also have to contend with the social, economic, and psychological dangers of performing that voluptuousness in the beauty hegemony that governs dominant American society.

Nevertheless, as Eduardo Bonilla-Silva (2006) shows, ideological rule is not absolute; even during periods of hegemonic rule, subordinate groups can develop oppositional views. They can deploy oppositional ideologies that challenge the commonsense nature of dominant ideologies and the social realities they create; by using alternative "racial ideologies" (Bonilla-Silva 2006, 9)—frames, ideas, and stories informed by their experiences as a subordinate group—marginalized people can and do challenge and defy regimes of power that seek to control them. Similarly, black Caribbean women do not acquiesce to the trajectories assigned to them in the global North because of their bodies. Their complicity with the "thick black woman" ideology impacts their participation in American society, but they do not necessarily accept this marginalization; they engage in "creative revelation" actions in which they construct discourses and perform behaviors that lead to their psychological well-being as well as new opportunities for participation in the United States.

The nature of the women's negotiations is largely informed by their identity narratives, how they construct their identities in the United States. As discussed in chapter 2, the first-generation women construct a permanent foreigner identity. In spite of having no desire to return to the Caribbean and having become naturalized citizens of the United States, these women resist claiming an American identity and deny any identification with American culture. They persistently position themselves and the Caribbean in opposition to the United States and non-Caribbean Americans. The second-generation women, on the other hand, develop flexible identities. They strategically construct their identities so as to advantageously position themselves in the United States. Therefore, while they embrace most norms and behaviors of their parents and the Caribbean, they distance themselves from what they (and Western societies) perceive as the "third world"-ness of the English-speaking Caribbean and align with American ideologies. In this way, the women are transcultural as they move between American and Caribbean cultures as it suits them.

Both the permanent foreigner and the flexible identity narratives help to facilitate the women's embodied cultural citizenship. Specifically, these narratives allow them to negotiate the dominant discourses about beauty in the United States and the Caribbean and challenge the negative physical capital and social and psychological issues their thick bodies accrue in their diasporic space. However, even as they create embodied cultural citizenship, the women simultaneously reinscribe imperialistic discourses about the Caribbean, the United States and their bodies.

Disrupting the Dominance of Thin

A significant part of the women's strategy to counter marginalization is the discourse of racialized beauty. As discussed in chapter 3, the women believe that their race is one of the most significant determinants of their bodily appearance and dictates their physical difference from American white women. Therefore, acceptance of the voluptuous aesthetic is largely associated with their racial identity; they believe that as black women, they should pursue the thick body. More than reflecting their racial identity, embracing what they perceive as the black aesthetic allows the participants to invert practices of exclusion and belonging and take an empowered stance in relation to the beauty discourses of the United States that deem them irrevocably unattractive. By embracing the "thick black woman," the women actively dismiss the dominant aesthetic of thinness and thus are not excluded from spaces of beauty (and acted upon by racist body politics) but rather have no desire to be included. In other words, their racial identification as black women allows them to destabilize the standardization of thinness (and whiteness) as the ultimate and only desirable beauty ideal.

The intersection of the discourses of race and beauty ideals in the women's responses also helps to construct a space where white culture is not revered. Colonialism and neocolonialism have bred Eurocentrism and the supremacy of Caucasian cultural forms, including language, dress, and racial schemas (Morley and Robins 1995). The discussions with the women reveal that body image in the black Caribbean diaspora does not follow this trend as the respondents do not value the "white aesthetic." Furthermore, unlike other spaces where occupying a black body is undesirable and dangerous (in American urban spaces, for example), their racial identification as black is advantageous in this context because it allows the women to create beauty discourses outside the dominant thin ideal and at least partially circumvent pressures to be thin.

Thickness and the Better Female Body

The women's racial-cultural veneration of voluptuousness also helps them reframe the thick body in beauty discourses of the United States. This is particularly true for women of the second generation. Similar to the fat pride movement (Murray 2005) as well as the attempts to reclaim the big black female body, second-generation women appropriate positive discourses about the thin body in U.S. society and apply them to their own. They undermine the primacy of thinness by contesting its validity as the epitome of femininity, beauty, and health and present their bigger bodies as the norm. Specifically, and contrary to the dominant beauty discourses prevalent in mainstream America, the women profess that there are more personal and social benefits to having a curvy body. Recall, for example, Evelyn, who characterizes her curvy body as more feminine. She says, "When I get big, I feel extra good about myself; I just feel like a woman. . . . I get that big confidence." In this way, she undercuts the discourses that position her curvy body as monstrous and outside the conception of femininity. Similarly, Debbie explains, "If I lose [my curves], I won't be confident. . . . I feel like the more body you have, men will pay more attention to you." Admittedly, her confidence is gained through heteronormative, patriarchal means (that is, through the attention of men), but by implying that men are uninterested in the thin body, Debbie challenges dominant ideas that link thinness to attractiveness.

Some women state that the black Caribbean ideal is more inclusive and thus more realistic and normal. The women openly discuss their frustration with trying to achieve a "Coca-Cola bottle" ideal that is imprecise and indefinable. However, this very characteristic of the black Caribbean interpretation of the thick body makes it more accessible to more women. They believe that this liminal body type (which exists between the axes of thin and fat) embraces a wider range of sizes; women with the voluptuous shape, whether on the larger side of the spectrum or on the thinner end, are acceptable. On the contrary, like many critics of the thin hegemony, they think that the American mainstream definition of attractiveness excludes most women. Being unequivocally grounded in thinness, which is judged by a thin frame and a small dress size, the thin system is inflexible and very difficult to attain. Women who do not fit into the accepted categories—who are not sufficiently slim or who do not fit into dress sizes 2 to 6—are deemed unattractive. In other words, the participants imply that the voluptuous ideal better accommodates the realities of women's bodies and is in fact more natural and regular.

Other women foreground the unrealistic and unhealthy eating and dieting practices that are associated with achieving the thin body. As Veniece explains, "There are so many things they have to do to get that skinny. They probably make themselves throw up, take pills, doing crack, who knows." Ronda also emphasizes the unrealistic and unhealthy habits fostered by the thin ideal, saying: "Say you wake up, you're hungry and you eat whatever, you are going to gain weight. . . . There is nothing wrong with that. That's normal. It makes sense. When you eat, you are going to gain weight. [In the United States] now, if you eat, they are going to say that you are eating too much. [They will say], 'You don't see that you're getting fat? Lose some weight! Go exercise! Go exercise!'" Here the women challenge the relationship between thinness, health, and normalcy that is propagated in mainstream society, highlighting the problematic practices needed to maintain what they see as an abnormal and ultimately unhealthy body aesthetic.

Furthermore, in a move that undermines the exclusive veneration of the thin body in the fashion industry, the women hold up the curvy body as the better silhouette and model for clothing. Quite simply, they believe that curvy bodies look better in clothes. Tony explains that when she sees thin women (in the media or otherwise), she criticizes their self-presentation. More precisely, she comments on how they look in their clothing, often concluding, "My [curvy] body would look better in that." Diane says she has no desire to be thin because of the risk of not being alluring when she dresses herself. She says: "When you so thin, things don't look right on you. To me, you have to have some shape; you have to have curves to make the clothes look right on you. . . . If you just skinny, you have nothing." Similarly, another participant, Pamela, explains her rationale for identifying with the bigger-body aesthetic of the Caribbean: "I am into fashion . . . so when you're too thin, your clothes hang on you; it doesn't fall a certain way. I am into silhouettes. So someone like Michelle Obama is the perfect size to me. She looks great in her dresses because of the size she is. If she was a size 00, she wouldn't look as good in those dresses. The European look doesn't work for me. I would never desire to be that." By touting this and other advantages of a curvy body, the women challenge the discourses circulating in contemporary U.S. society that associate thinness with femininity, normalcy, style, and ultimately positive physical capital.

The mobilization of racial and cultural discourses has ambivalent results for the women's embodied cultural citizenship, however. In spite of the positive body image that the women engender by reframing the thick black body, the discourses employed in this recasting concurrently subvert and reinscribe their negative physical capital in the United States. In other words, while successful in maintaining the women's self-esteem, their inversion of thin and thick ideologies does not make their bodies more accepted in American society.

First, and as discussed in chapter 3, the women's articulation of the racialization of beauty aesthetics feeds into the existing beauty hegemony of the United States. While they did not create the voluptuous figure (which many black women have), European discourses played a significant role in constructing the idea that all black women are big as a means to mark them as valueless in the project of modernity; the "thick black woman" ideology was propagated by white colonialists with the purpose of othering and marginalizing them. Granted, African and African diaspora cultures have reclaimed, reframed, and elevated the curvaceous black woman. However, this image of black femininity (the always already thick black woman), when understood within the context of the discursive terrain of colonialism, cannot be completely separated from its history in imperialistic designs. The standardization of the "thick black woman," the construction of this singular body type for black women, was (and still is) used to characterize all black women and to justify their devaluation in modern spaces. In other words, the trope of the "Hottentot Venus," the voluptuous (read erotic and wild) black woman, is embedded in the "thick black woman" ideology, which is used to uphold gendered racial inequality in the United States.

As evidenced by reports from the women in this study, black women of this body type are marginalized in mainstream society and suffer indignities in the United States: they are treated as spectacles in public spaces, they have their bodies liberally and constantly critiqued, and they are relegated to a few clothing choices. So while black Caribbean women's endorsement of the voluptuous body as the better aesthetic is empowering in one sense (as it reappropriates and redefines black femininity), it at least partially feeds and plays into strategies of domination. Therefore, the women's racial and cultural beliefs are dialectical in their negotiations of embodied cultural citizenship; they provide ways for the women to attain confidence in the United States, but they also lead the women to rehearse discourses and practices that perpetuate their marginalization and erasure.

Performativity, Mimicry, and Dress

Another prominent strategy that emerges among women of both generations is performativity. These women employ cultural ideologies of performance to create embodied cultural citizenship; they mobilize discourses of self-presentation and engage in practices and enactments (informed by their cultural location) to position their bodies in ways that challenge their subordination.

Within sociological discussions of identity formation, performativity and performance theory argue that identities are not essentialized but are performative, at least partially constructed through specific types of self-presentation. They are the result of repeated, social (shared) human actions (Warren and Fassett 2011). These bodily acts and "stylization of the body" can be subversive to hegemonic norms, specifically when performed as an alternative to the existing dominant notions of (gendered) identity (Butler 1999, 43, 44); they can undermine the claim to naturalness purported by hegemonic norms.[1] Marlon Bailey illustrates this subversive potential in his study of gay black ballroom culture in Detroit. He posits that "performance makes it possible to revise, negotiate, and reconstitute gender and sexual categories and norms," which enables participants to "reconfigure gender and sexual roles and relations while constructing a more open minoritarian social sphere" (2013, 18).

Postcolonial women living within and under the imperialistic structures of a Western power engage in such performances to challenge existing ideologies, performances that (ironically) entail copying colonial discourses of body politics and self-presentations. While it is tempting to interpret these imitations as solely the product of self-hatred and the internalization of oppressive regimes, Homi Bhabha (1994) suggests that this "mimicry" is ambivalent: it resembles the colonizers culture (and thus at least partially reinscribes it), but when enacted by "inappropriate," othered bodies, it also creates a mocking and threatening presence (a "menace") that disrupts the authority of the imperial power. For example, Janell Hobson describes how "Set Girls" in Jamaican slave carnivals danced and paraded in decorative high fashion "parodying notions of 'European' ladylike behavior" but also "challeng[ing] their impoverished state as enslaved women" (2005, 91). Jenny Sharpe (2002) also demonstrates how slave concubines deflected their sexual exploitation by mimicking white domesticity. She argues that these women performed domestic duties that are reserved for white women—such as being surrogate mothers for white children and sexual partners for white men—to gain agency in a system that they were powerless to change. They seemingly acquiesced to the rules, rituals, and laws imposed by slavery, systems that were designed to maintain their subjugation, but manipulated them to their own ends.

Such tactical moves are often dismissed as assimilatory and not radical enough to be perceived as oppositional. Yet they enabled black women to gain agency and empowerment in moments of subjugation. As Sharpe (2002) states, this form of performative resistance exceeds strictly defined rules of opposition and complicity. These acts do not completely dismantle existing systems, but they allow the women to undermine their oppression and marginalization. As Judith Butler says, such performativity is "not freedom, but a question of how to work the trap that one is inevitably in" (1992, 84). Mimicry of dominant body politics may thus be a site of intervention that challenges (though does not dismantle) axes of legitimacy. In other words, through mimicry, the body of the black Caribbean woman becomes a "third space" that reinterprets and re-presents, but does not fully evade, the beauty ideals and expectations of the cultural spheres it straddles.

Women of both the first and the second generation mobilize and rely on performativity and mimicry to create such empowering spaces and sustain themselves in the United States. Specifically, the women deploy performances of respectability and Americanness to contend with their negative physical capital and social and psychological struggles.

Caribbean Respectability, Dress, and Physical Beauty
For women of the first generation (particularly the older ones), the performance of respectability is prominent in their negotiations of body image disturbances and social hierarchies.

Respectability refers to a set of understood ideas (proscriptions) on how one should behave in public spaces. It includes rules on how one should speak, move, dress and interact with others in public. According to Peter Wilson (1995), all societies in the English-speaking Caribbean are oriented to a value system of respectability, which, owing to their colonial histories, supports the superiority of Euro-American culture and the class structures created under colonial rule. This respectability is thus defined through the performance and display of elements and qualities associated with the upper and middle classes of Europe and America and their counterparts in the islands. As such, it is largely predicated on wealth, but wealth alone does not determine respectability. A respectable person uses "proper" (British) English, exhibits formal table manners and general politeness, maintains a restrained demeanor, and has a monogamous marriage. Such a person also attains higher education and subsequently is employed in a profession that is well respected in society. Furthermore, a respectable person follows a standard of dress, conduct, and lifestyle that aligns with white, Euro-American ideals of modesty, restraint, discipline, and purity (Wilson 1995). Moreover, all these elements are closely related to morality. In sum, respectability in the Anglophone Caribbean is a class-, race-, and nation-coded cultural discourse meant to reinforce hierarchies and police boundaries of acceptable citizenship.

The use of respectability to create and maintain social hierarchies is a significant feature in the postcolonial contexts of the Caribbean. In countries such as Jamaica, for example, postcolonial elites tried to create a sense of nationalism by promoting a particular brand of Jamaicanness based on, among other values, respectability (Thomas 2004). This respectability was premised on a middle-class Jamaican Creole sensibility that conceived of blackness (and Africanness) as inferior and the idea that one could "correct" one's blackness through the performance of civility (Thame 2011a). In this system, poor and working-class black Jamaicans were perceived as the least respectable due to the intersection of their race and class. Respectability also has a particularly ambivalent and problematic place in black communities in general, as it has been used as a way to uplift and elevate black people but also as a tool to promote white middle-class sensibilities and vilify poor and working-class black people; by creating rules that essentially police black people, this politics of respectability actually further pathologizes blackness and black culture, indicating that left alone, black people are always already uncivil. There is also a very distinct gender undercurrent, as most of the rules are directed at black women and their sexuality and what may be described as the containment of their bodies.

Wilson contrasts the ideal of respectability with reputation, "an opposing but politically subordinate value complex through which individuals can achieve a measure of existential fulfillment and recognition outside of the strictures of respectability" (1995, 116). Reputation, as he sees it, is a counterculture to respectability in that it is available to the vast majority of black, low-income people of the Caribbean, who are excluded from the system of respectability. Rather than being based on class and the performance of middle-class status, reputation is more relational, more egalitarian, and values honorable lived experiences and conduct that are recognized by peers. In other words, reputation is earned and bestowed, as opposed to given as a birthright.

The first-generation women in the study draw on respectability in their negotiation of embodied cultural citizenship. Although many of them would have been excluded from respectability in their societies because of their color (dark skin) and class, they mobilize this value system in the United States to invert cultural discourses that position them as inferior because of their body type. Specifically, they perform respectability through stansdards of dress to claim difference from and superiority to Americans.

For these participants, well-fitting clothing is crucial to denoting respectability; regardless of their size and shape, it is imperative for women to clothe themselves in a manner that flatters the types of bodies that they have and that reflects their social position. The style or type of the clothing is not important, so long as it is appropriate for the wearer's body type, age, and social roles and is worn on the proper occasion. Therefore, while the women speak openly about their ideal of a voluptuous body and the dissatisfactions they have with their own, what they put on their bodies is just as important to them as actual body size and shape. Marsha says, "I put on my clothes, I look good, and I always say, 'As long as [your] clothes is clean, and you looking good, [be confident].'" Here she implies that wearing pristine garments (a signifier of good hygiene, a good household, and high class) in public gives her confidence in spite of other shortcomings with her body. In this way, the participants' discussion of clothing choices and the public presentation of bodies centers the notion of respectability in discourses of body politics; they imply that how the body is presented and what it projects to others are just as important as the body itself. By emphasizing respectable self-presentation, the participants undermine pressures to fulfill a physical beauty ideal and contest the authority of standards that they do not meet; they reframe personal value as deriving from decency and morality (as represented through dress), and not from body size, race, or class.

The women not only uphold this standard of dress for themselves but use it to judge the morals and respectability of women in their diasporic space. Dress has moral significance for them because, more than the actual size and shape of the bodies themselves, clothing choice is used to connote self-worth, integrity of character, and respectability. For these women, wearing clothing that does not adequately conceal what they deem unsightly body parts (such as big stomachs or sagging arms), clothing that, in their estimation, exposes too much, or that they consider inappropriate for one's age is indicative of defective upbringing and degenerate cultural values. As one respondent, Shera, says about women (particularly Latinas) in her neighborhood, "They put on little kid's stuff, and think that they look cute coming out, and they could be having kids with them, and they looking just like that." Janet also had this to say about the scantily clad women she encounters in her neighborhood: "It come to their background. They used to that thing. . . . Like, I would walk on White Plains Road, and then I'll see women in my age group [forty-eight], and I'd be like, 'Oh my goodness, they need to stop,' but that's them, you know.[2] I wouldn't be caught in the rain like that cause I wasn't brought up that way, and I didn't grow my children that way either."

Both of these participants (and others in the research study) use their own politics of dress to disparage the women in their communities in the United States. They regard those who do not meet their standards or those who hold other ideologies as being of inferior character. So the discourse of respectability through dress allows black Caribbean women to claim superiority over other women in their social environment in New York City. By presenting respectable dress as a quintessential element of value in society, the women bring postcolonial sensibility to bear on their diasporic space; they deploy it to neutralize the privileges afforded to women with the "right" body in U.S. and black Caribbean societies and assuage their own feelings of exclusion.

Moreover, by emphasizing dress and individual public display, the participants highlight the performative nature of morality. Their statements explicitly express the idea that how one behaves, speaks, and dresses (not the actual body) are indicators of one's respectability, morality, and decency. This idea challenges the Platonic concept of *kalokagatheia*, which identifies a direct relationship between physical beauty and inner beauty, the belief that one's physical appearance is an indication of the goodness of one's morals (Wegenstein 2012). The beauty-morality relationship constructed by Plato has taken on various articulations over time and has been mobilized for various ends. Physiognomists, for example, used it as the foundation to create tools for deconstructing female beauty, and racist theorists employed it to demonize, criminalize, and ultimately erase nonwhite races.

Plato's *kalokagatheia* underscores much of the discourses of beauty and cosmetic improvements currently circulating in the twenty-first century. In the contemporary rhetoric of beauty, people, particularly women, are encouraged to work on their "ugly" bodies as a way to better reflect their inner essence and are told that only people with certain inner, psychological characteristics (such as willpower and passion) are deserving of such bodily change (Wegenstein 2012). The first-generation women, however, undermine this link between body and character, which implies that decency and morality are innate and natural ("you are born that way"). Instead, by mobilizing the rhetoric of respectable dress, they present the idea that the body itself does not naturally determine morality and morality is not intrinsic but can be constructed through self-presentation.

Interestingly, however, performing respectability through clothing seems to become important only after failed attempts to attain the desired body ideal, indicating that the women do not fully eschew the ideologies of bodies and social worth that are pervasive in their diasporic space. For example, Shera, who criticizes the Latinas in her neighborhood, also states: "No matter how many hours you exercise or change the diet, you just reach a plateau when you lose no more weight and you just have to come to grips and accept yourself, you know, and dress yourself appropriately." For her, the perfect scenario is to achieve the desired body size and shape, but when all body improvement projects have failed, women should accept their bodies and dress in a manner that connotes propriety and respectability.

The women themselves also employ clothing to perform the thick ideal. Sue, for example, speaks about wearing minimizers to give the illusion of smaller breasts (the part of her body that violates the "Coca-Cola bottle" shape). Natalie, a petite respondent, also implies that when she was not gaining weight, she wore padded bras and other clothing that would augment her small frame. So even though they consider themselves morally superior to other women because of their propriety in dress, their responses indicate underlying anxieties about their body size; they highlight their lingering desires to create the "Coca-Cola bottle" body that makes them pleasing in their community in the United States. Therefore, as the women deploy ideas of respectability to contest hegemonic ideas of physical beauty that center the body, they also employ dress as a tool to create the hegemonic body type of the black Caribbean community.

Dress, Style, and Being American
The second-generation participants also disrupt beauty hierarchies through performativity, though in a manner that differs from that of their first-generation counterparts. As discussed in chapter 2, this cohort of women create flexible identities; they claim a black Caribbean cultural identity but frequently align themselves with the United States when it proves personally beneficial to them. This flexible identity informs their body politics, as they strategically perform Americanness through clothing choices. In other words, they take on and mimic mainstream American culture in their self-presentation and so align themselves with American sensibilities to counter negative physical capital and challenges to their body image.

The participants do not holistically embrace black Caribbean body politics. They admire and uphold the thick body as the ideal body type, but they pursue American style of dress. Similar to their first-generation counterparts, they frequently raise the topic of good self-presentation. This includes aspects of respectability, that is, dressing tastefully in clothing that is not ill fitting. However, for the second-generation women, it also means dressing fashionably, carefully choosing clothing and accessories according to how they work or look together. The ensembles do not have to be expensive, but they must be put together in a manner that reflects current fashion trends as well as individual fashion sense. For these women, it is not simply dressing or looking like everybody else but rather using contemporary trends and fashions for ideas about how to create their own style; it is about using fashion as a visual representation of themselves. So while the first-generation women speak about dress in the context of morals and respectability, the second-generation women predominantly discuss dress in the context of style and being "in fashion."

The women's styles vary based on their unique personalities and desired self-presentation, but they are all inspired by U.S. fashion; they do not believe that looking good can be accomplished by donning what they describe as Caribbean modes of dress. Therefore, the adornment of their bodies—their hairstyles, outfits, shoes, piercings, and accessories— reflects the dominant trends of the United States, specifically those circulating in New York City. In fact, the women actively seek out American fashion trends and openly dismiss and disparage the fashion styles they believe are found among black Caribbean people. In reality, black Caribbean mainstream fashion is very similar to that found in the United States, but the women perceive a vast difference between the two.

For example, when asked why she prefers American fashion, Karrie confesses: "I don't think Jamaicans are stylish. Their style is just not up to par with me: too many colors . . . too much accessories. . . . They just look cheap. The colors bother me. The big bangles and the costume jewelry bother me. . . . With them, it's just all over the place. It's just cheap. . . . If I were to go to Jamaica today, they would know I'm from *fahrin* [the United States]." Even though she, like other second-generation participants, self-identifies as black Caribbean, her statement explicitly delineates clear differences in taste between herself and Jamaicans born in or living on the island. In fact, the image of the inexpensive, brightly colored clothing and oversized accessories recuperates Western depictions and conceptions of "third world," "island people" whose fun-loving nature is given to excesses of all kinds, including dress. Karrie, who deploys her black

Caribbean identity in the United States in the process of self-exoticization, now distances herself from the "third world" conception of the Caribbean by deliberately and blatantly grounding her own style in American, "first world" trends and vogues.

Tony also says: "Of course we prefer our culture, but style-wise, [no]. When you think about it, especially with Jamaica, they always want us [living in the United States] to send them stuff. They don't know nothing [about fashion]. They like, 'Whatever you all send, we wear.' . . . I feel like they have style when they come here. In Jamaica I don't really see much, because most of the time it's clothes that we send them." Her friend Veniece also says, "In St. Vincent, it's hot down there, so they just wear whatever to be comfortable. We over here, we dress to look nice." In other words "island people" are less concerned with style and the urbane, refined aspects of self-presentation. Another participant, Sandy, remarks on the outdatedness of Jamaican fashion. She says, "The fashion in Jamaica is backwards in the sense of some things that were hot [popular] up here a year ago, is crazy [popular] down there right now." She later adds that the industry is becoming more up to date but is still largely dependent on American trends and thus remains passé. For these women, then, the clothing and looks of the Caribbean are outdated, inexpensive, unoriginal, unmodern impersonations of American trends.

Evidently, while the women's ideal body type favors that which is promoted in the black Caribbean community, they choose to dress and present their bodies according to American and European standards. In doing so, I believe they counter the negative physical capital they may accrue in the United States. As Bernadette Wegenstein (2012) demonstrates, everyone from employers to potential mates employ the Platonic concept of *kalokagatheia* in that they use visible attributes of the body to judge the "health" and thus goodness of perspective employees and companions. People who do not "look the part," who have neither the body desired in contemporary society (that is, Euro-American, white, middle class), are marginalized and excluded from the global economy. Black Caribbean women are often marginalized and demoralized in the United

States because of their deviant voluptuous bodies that do not conform to the sanctioned thin aesthetic of mainstream America; as women who maintain and desire curvy bodies, they are marked as grotesque and not very valuable to the project of modernity.

However, dressing their bodies to mimic the self-presentation of the colonial powers disrupts monolithic ideas about race and bodies and creates new opportunities for social and economic engagement in American society (and by extension, the global economy). Clothing is a large part of creating a "healthy" look, as style and fashion are routinely used to assess the modernity, cosmopolitanism, taste, social status, and the overall well-being, goodness, and value of a person. By draping their "aberrant" bodies in fashions approved by the U.S. mainstream, these second-generation women circumvent the negative physical capital created by their thick bodies. Their American performance of style is thus a form of cultural capital (Bourdieu 1986), which facilitates their acceptance and entrance into spaces in the United States that would have otherwise been closed to them because of their race, nationality, and the shape and size of their bodies. They may not have the "correct" body aesthetic, but they are fashionable and stylish in ways that are acceptable in the American context, and on this basis, they are not completely marginalized. Their performance and mimicry of American clothing are a critical means through which they negotiate oppressive regimes of body politics in the United States.

Furthermore, similar to women of the first generation, by emphasizing the importance of self-presentation, the women minimize and circumvent the pressure to maintain a perfect body. They revise the conception of beauty to include personal style, so that neither the thin nor the voluptuous figure is the only significant criterion of femininity. Diane, who is relatively thin and does not have the ideal black Caribbean body, makes up for this perceived lack by referring to her dress and style. She says: "I don't have big breasts and I am fine with that. I look good in jeans and dresses. I like to wear dresses that print out my figure. . . . I dress up and I feel like myself. . . . I put on some heels, some makeup, and that's me. I feel confident." Pamela also says, "There are certain body areas that I am not happy with, but I clothe it well."

The hybridization of black Caribbean body aesthetics and mainstream American modes of self-presentation allows the women to undermine the negative physical capital and challenges to self-image created by the beauty hegemonies of both the United States and the Anglophone Caribbean. In this way, the women's everyday decisions around fashion are mimicries that help them navigate the negative effects of living in these beauty regimes. They capitulate to American standards, but in doing so with their nonmainstream bodies, they construct embodied cultural citizenship.

This performance is not wholly emancipatory, as it entails reproduction of oppressive conventions, as discussed earlier; it is an attempt to resituate the black female body within a "Euro-feminine realm" (Shaw 2006, 150). Furthermore, it requires a lot of effort to keep up with these looks. The women have to be willing to invest the time to do research and remain current in the trends. More importantly, the women's performance of the ideal black Caribbean body and mimicry of Eurocentric styles are predicated on consumption; they need to have the resources (access to the Internet and various social platforms, for example) and the funds to purchase the clothes, accessories, and services necessary to create and maintain "the look." In other words, their negotiations are rooted in the ethos of consumerism.

According to Leslie Sklair (1995), Western societies have created and propagated a culture-ideology of consumerism that promotes the purchase of objects to satisfy wants and give meaning to life. This form of consumerism is grounded in individual self-interest and accumulation of private wealth. The cosmetics and fashion industries, for example, have long employed the culture-ideology of consumerism to market their products, reinforcing the myth that consumption of feminine beauty aids can be a corrective to individual social and embodied ills. Consumer culture thus allows for, and encourages, individual difference and empowerment but obscures structural hierarchies and forestalls collective strategies for social change; it prioritizes "commodity purchases above more ambitious goals such as decentering the role of beauty in women's lives" (Johnston and Taylor 2008, 960–61).

In other words, consumerism's emphasis on personal fulfillment conceals the fundamental mechanisms and structures of capitalist exploitation and minimizes attempts at collective mobilization and systemic change. The participants' appeal to consumerism therefore privileges personal empowerment ahead of collective, overall change to the system. In this sense, the women's individual negotiations cannot and do not overthrow or dismantle the "master's house" (Lorde 2007), the beauty-society hegemony. Instead, these individual, personal performances and mimicries are subversive acts that breed self-empowerment and make daily life more dignified and sustainable.

Moreover, the women's conceptualization of Caribbean fashion is problematic, as it reflects dominant perceptions of the region as a whole. More specifically, their perception of black Caribbean styles emphasizes the position of the Caribbean in the global economy. It reinforces the "globalist geo-temporal politics" (Chow 2013, 101) that positions the Caribbean and its cultures as lagging behind in contrast to the advanced, dynamic environment of the United States. Furthermore, it highlights the dependency of the Caribbean on the United States. Largely due to its proximity to the United States as well as global neocolonialist policies and agendas, the Caribbean relies on the United States for information, resources, and trade (Sheller 2003). The description of black Caribbean fashion propagated by the respondents rehearses the perceived underdevelopment of black Caribbean industries and draws attention to these structures of dependency that characterize the relationship between the Caribbean and the United States.

Thus, the appropriation of American styles facilitates the women's personal maneuverability in beauty regimes but simultaneously underscores imperialist discourses about black Caribbean people and the Caribbean collectively; it allows for some individual empowerment but undermines *collective* advancements in geopolitical systems of domination. Said differently, Eurocentric ideologies about the Caribbean enable and are enabled by the women's flexible identity; these ideas about the region figure largely into their politics of fashion, and thus, while allowing them to personally position themselves more favorably in the United States, their disassociation from Caribbean styles ultimately reinforces those ideas.

Privileging the Whole Self

Finally, the women counteract challenges to their self-image by emphasizing personal well-being and achievements.

Respectability and the Construction of Selfhood

The first-generation women, who draw on ideas of respectable dress to counteract notions of their deficient morality, also mobilize elements of respectability to emphasize their worth as women beyond their outward appearance. Specifically, these women employ discourses related to their sociocultural positions; they draw on various noncorporeal facets of their identities to assuage the pressures, disappointments, and anxieties that accompany the quest for the "thick black woman" ideal as well as the double-consciousness fostered by living within the thin hegemony. In other words, they foreground positive embodied experiences and accomplishments that constitute them as *valuable* persons without using their body size and shape as the standard.

For example, the college-educated women in this group emphasize the significance of erudition. They believe that education supersedes appearance as a tool of advancement and social status. The women posit the development of the mind, not the body, as important to social and economic mobility. In fact, some of the women imply that only uneducated women feel the need to adamantly pursue beauty ideals because their bodies are their only social currency. One participant, Sheryl, says: "Being pretty does not get you anywhere; education get you everywhere."

Admittedly, the college-educated women in the group confess to participating in body-enhancing projects, demonstrating that, despite their erudition, they still pursue the black Caribbean ideal. Furthermore, this rhetoric recuperates elitist, classist ideologies that position black

Caribbean women with no college education as intellectually useless. Moreover, this discourse relies heavily on the Eurocentric separation of mind and body, which implies that focus on the body is indicative of lesser mental capacities. However, for black women from the global South, using the rhetoric of education is a radical move that trains focus on their intellect, not their bodies.

Many of the women also highlight the significance of other markers of dominant femininity, such as marriage and motherhood. They believe that only unmarried women and women without children need to live up to the ideal. The idea is that women who already have significant others do not have as much pressure to cultivate the ideal body since they are already attached, and women who have borne children have a noble reason for their "bad" shape and are therefore excused. Martha, one of the mothers in the study, states:

> I have a tummy, but I have an excuse; I have two children. . . . I don't have perky breasts because I breast-fed two children. Overall, I am happy with my body. . . . There was a song a few years ago called "Tuk in Yuh Belly" [Suck in Your Stomach]. . . . In essence what these guys were saying, "If you have children, you do not need to make excuses for your stomach and your breast; you have gone through the child-bearing process. We know what nine months can do to the body for a lifetime so don't feel bad."

By suggesting that married (or unavailable) women and women with children (or undesirable women) do not have to align themselves with the dominant standards of beauty, the women reinforce the patriarchal idea that women's bodies are primarily for the consumption of others, and function to attract men. Nevertheless, some of the women use their social positions of wife and mother, the noblest and most respected accomplishments in dominant discourses of Caribbean womanhood, to highlight and underscore the idea that their value is not contingent on the thickness or thinness of their bodies.

Some participants also present their breadwinning role as an important element in their personhood and communities. Specifically, some respondents highlight their responsibility to care for their families in their homelands as the main reason why they cannot and should not be expected to maintain the desirable body. Shaunie says: "Our families on the island believe that because we are in America we are in a better position financially. We then have the additional stress of supporting our families back home on the island. . . . We feel responsible for our families. We squeeze ourselves here and sacrifice so that we can support them." She later acknowledges that body sculpting is one of the major sacrifices that immigrants make, a fact that is most obvious when they return to their homelands and find that their relatives and friends actually look better than they who left their islands to live a "better life." Catherine similarly highlights the black Caribbean immigrant experience as defense for her body. She says, "We are stressed because we have two and three jobs. . . . We are trying to maintain here and [back home]."

These women thus imply that they could achieve the curvaceous ideal under different circumstances. However, their current immigrant lifestyle, preoccupied with working and assuming the financial responsibility for multiple households, requires that they privilege gainful employment over obsessive attention to appearance. In fact, this role of breadwinner is not new to them; while dominant, middle-class Western ontologies view this as a conventionally masculine discourse and role, black women in the Caribbean have historically assumed the role of provider in their homes (Wilcot 1995). By deploying these discourses, the women thus radically challenge Western patriarchal views of women's roles in the home and society. They also refocus attention to their reputation as good, sacrificial providers and minimize (even put to shame) any reference to the condition of their bodies. In doing so, they provide a counterclaim to the notion that they are dispensable economic subjects and challenge hegemonic definitions of femininity that locate it primarily in whiteness and domesticity.

Other women employ discourses of maturity (and wisdom). Sue, who is in her early fifties, explains:

This is my philosophy: when you're in your teens, like seventeen, eighteen, you gotta be small, everything has to be tight. When you get in your twenties, that's the dumb stage because everything is like oh I have to [fix myself up]. . . . But when you get to be in your thirties, you start to view your body differently, you know; you still wanna be hip and down, but you view your body differently. . . . You try to be conservative, and you say I gotta go to the gym now and gotta tuck it back like I was in my twenties and, you know. My thing is, over the years, I've just learnt more about me, what makes me comfortable. . . . It's only what makes me comfortable.

For her, trying to live up to the beauty ideals of society is a preoccupation of youth; she implies that as women mature, they should be less concerned with gratifying others and be more introspective and accepting of their bodies. Another respondent concurs, stating, "We are all growing and evolving. I couldn't be 125 [pounds] my entire life."

The women's emphasis on education, motherhood, marital status, financial responsibilities, and other social positions are closely tied to the performance of respectability promoted in Anglophone Caribbean societies. As Wilson (1995) has highlighted, education, monogamy, a nuclear family, and gainful employment are all pillars of morality in the English-speaking Caribbean. Recuperation of the logic of respectability is problematic for it is based on the rules, rituals, and laws imposed by former colonizers to maintain class and racial hierarchies and ultimately secure the subjugation of poor and working-class black people (particularly women) in the Caribbean.

However, while problematic, these discourses challenge popular conceptions of black Caribbean women. Eurocentric ontology locates their value(lessness) in their bodies and dictates that as black women, particularly of the working class, they are not worth much, as evidenced by their bigger bodies. By shifting focus away from the shape and size of the body and toward personal accomplishments, duties, and integrity, the women engage in an ontological reorientation; they change the location of their worth (and those of other black women) from their bodies to their lived experiences and what they have accomplished. They indicate that size does not define them, thus creating alternative criteria for inclusion in black Caribbean and American spaces; they may not have the "right" body, but they are educated and responsible and therefore valuable members of society. The discourses of social positions are not entirely liberatory, but they allow the women to reimagine themselves outside the dominant paradigms constructed for them and to negotiate their position in dominant American and black Caribbean societies.

Self-Love and the Construction of Selfhood

The women of the second generation also take steps to privilege a more holistic selfhood and undermine the importance of the body in discourses of subjectivity. Specifically, they co-opt the American mantra of self-love and self-acceptance to undermine emphasis on achieving the bodies endorsed by the black Caribbean and U.S. beauty regimes. Many of the women say that above pursuing and maintaining the ideal body sanctioned by either the black Caribbean or American culture, they want to be healthy. For them, healthy is defined not as being overly concerned with attaining the perfect body (and thus looking outward) but as pursuing the size and shape that is right for each of them. This healthy of which they speak is individualized; it is not represented by a specific, global body type. While they believe that the bigger black Caribbean aesthetic is better than the dominant American standard of thinness, they also imply that obsession with either ideal is detrimental and unhealthy. In sum, the healthy body is one that is not dictated by society but is in line with each woman's self-reflection, self-knowledge, and self-possession; it is a body derived from empowerment of the self.

Sandy, who suffered from eating disorders in the pursuit of thinness and who currently contends with copious comments about her bigger size, now embraces a "healthy and happy body" mantra. For her, healthy does not have a particular look. She says: "It's just whatever you're happy with, and whatever you're content with. . . . I was so focused on being tiny and now I couldn't care less. . . . I'm experiencing a time right now where I don't care about my size. I am delivering myself from my body dysmorphic syndrome, saying whatever happens, happens. . . . I have gotten to the point where I really don't care." Admittedly, she embraces this rhetoric after failed attempts to acquire the ideal American body, but her statement reveals an attitude of self-empowerment that can release her from the neurosis created by racist, classist, and patriarchal beauty regimes. Sandra similarly promotes ideas of self-trust and self-love when she describes her ideal body as one that feels right to her. She says: "To some people, I would be very skinny . . . and to other people, I'm big. . . . I know when I am uncomfortable with how my body feels. . . . When I am exercising, I want to get to a point where I am okay and then maintain that. I am not trying to compete with society's image; that's too much for me. I just want to find a healthy balance."

The rhetoric of good health that permeates the women's discussions is reminiscent of contemporary public discourses surrounding weight loss and self-improvement projects in the United States. Rationale for pursuing a slim(mer) body is often couched in the idea of being healthy; weight-loss programs and promotions are replete with the suggestion that smaller bodies are equivalent to healthier lifestyles and thus present weight loss not as a beautification project but as a means to becoming healthy. In fact, Wegenstein (2012) discusses how the desire to be perceived as "health conscious" and to achieve the "healthy look" are informing women's and men's decisions to undergo cosmetic surgery. In this way, the trope of good health is employed as a strategy to uphold and advance the thin aesthetic of the United States. The women in the study also mobilize and mimic the discourse of health in relation to their body image. However, instead of using it to support a thinner body, they use it to promote self-empowerment. The rhetoric allows the women to negotiate the obsession and neurosis created by black Caribbean and American cultural expectations of their bodies.

Collectively, both generations of women challenge the Platonic rule of *kalokagatheia*, which governs contemporary discourses of beauty. The standards of beauty of both the United States and the black Caribbean emphasize the visible aspects of a person and posit that by pursuing and maintaining an ideal body, women can achieve social, economic, and psychological success. Women whose bodies do not reflect the archetypes of these systems are excluded from the social and economic life of their respective societies. Through discourses of social position and self-love, the women decenter the role of outward appearance in their lives and expand the conception of beauty and success beyond their bodies.

A Word on Using the Master's Tools

Audre Lorde (2007) cautions that women should not seek to gain empowerment by using the same strategies that have been used to marginalize and oppress them. She argues that "the master's tools will never dismantle the master's house. They may allow us temporarily to beat him at his own game, but they will never enable us to bring about genuine change" (2007, 112). The women in this study deploy several of the "master's tools" in their struggle with and against the beauty-society hegemony they face in the United States; they appropriate and mimic dominant discourses and practices that are meant to exclude them as a way to negotiate their inclusion into American and black Caribbean societies. As Lorde predicts, while these tactics allow them some maneuverability, they do not topple the hegemony, and thus they are suspect as effective redemptive mechanisms.

Notwithstanding, everyday acts of resistances and negotiations, such as these done by both the first- and second-generation women, are more than signs of individual agency; they signal the political consciousness of the women, their knowledge and acknowledgment of societal inequalities and a desire to challenge them (Thompson 2014). Furthermore, this everyday embodied resistance is an important part of the women's decolonization project, which entails changing and reframing how they view themselves, challenging the internalization of self-hatred, and reclaiming humanity. As Maziki Thame states (referencing Henry 2002): "If colonialism is depersonalizing, decolonization must involve reclaiming humanity" (2011b, 83). Part of this rehumanizing project for postcolonial black Caribbean immigrant women entails raising their self-esteem, freeing themselves from the inferiority complex created by neocolonial body politics that mark them as unattractive and useless in the global economy; it involves reversing colonialism's assumptions about their "monstrosity" and valuelessness in the modern world. The respondents' personal embodied negotiations indicate the initiation of such a project.

Critically Engaging the Media

Media are the primary vehicles through which discourses of the beauty hegemony are maintained and propagated in the United States and are the main ways in which the women are "hailed" into the system (Althusser 1971). As demonstrated in chapter 3, popular culture is important in cultivating and sustaining black Caribbean women's "romance" with the voluptuous ideal. Black Caribbean popular culture help to shape the way that these women construct and perform beauty; they normalize and reify the dominant ideology of the voluptuous black woman and remind women in the diaspora of what is expected of their bodies. These media subsequently contribute to the women's discontent with bodies that do not fit the curvy ideal. Additionally, by repeatedly foregrounding voluptuous black female bodies in music videos and lyrics, television series, and magazines, American mainstream media concurrently reinforce the ideology of the "thick black woman" and normalize negative responses to that voluptuous body type. American media thus create a thin hegemony that complicates these black Caribbean immigrant women's self-esteem and their ability to transgress or circumvent discourses and practices that marginalize them.

Nevertheless, in spite of the power of media to socialize these women into beauty hegemonies, the openness of media texts allow for insertions and interpretations that go against the dominant, hegemonic messages; while they limit interpretations, media texts do not determine or control how the women respond to representations of beauty and how they are incorporated into their everyday consciousness. Some of the women deny any influence of media on their lives, supporting literature on the third-person effect of media (Davison 1983). However, their overall responses divulge a more complicated relationship to media, one that is ambivalent, and one that, I argue, helps to inform how they negotiate the very beauty hegemony that media uphold. Their interactions with the media thus involve engaging in discursive tactics to contend with and evade the controlling images and discourses they encounter.

Cultural studies scholars have explored this issue of counterhegemony and agency in audiences. In his seminal work, Stuart Hall (1980) posits that cultural texts perpetuate the normative standards established by the dominant class through the dissemination of "preferred meanings." Nevertheless, the "encoded" message and the audience's interpretation of that message is often asymmetrical, as audiences have liberty to accept the intended message, accept part of that message, or reject the message entirely; that is, they may engage in dominant-hegemonic, negotiated, or oppositional readings, respectively.[3] The disparity between the intended message and its interpretation occurs because, contrary to previous theories that ignored the heterogeneity of audiences, persons do not receive and engage with media messages in the same way.[4] Rather, the ideological positions held by individual viewers and listeners moderate their interaction and acceptance of the desired message. In other words, sociocultural factors (such as race, gender, ethnicity, nationality, and even body politics) shape the perspectives and experiences of audience members and mitigate their interaction with and acceptance of media texts. Hall's theory illuminates the ideological struggle that characterizes engagement with media texts; this activity is never a passive act of consumption but rather one that entails subject-making strategies and exercises of agency by audience members, replicating the struggles that occur in nonmediated experiences.

In order to capture the ideological struggles that occur around interactions with the media, we need to refine our definition of media engagement, looking beyond the actual moment of watching or reading to those nonmediated instances when media are still being engaged. As Ien Ang (1996) states, we need "radically contextualized" ethnographies in audience studies that endorse a more holistic definition (and analysis) of media engagement that captures what is consumed, how it is consumed, and the factors that inform its application to everyday life. Robin Means Coleman (2002) underscores this point, highlighting how media engagement is embedded in other everyday practices that moderate how audiences read, negotiate, and apply mediated messages. Analogously, Larry Strelitz (2002) states that scholars should examine media consumption in relation to other cultural experiences that moderate media messages. He has found that social location and networks influence media consumption patterns and identity formation; the social group that his subjects' identified with informed what they desired from and how they interpreted media.

These scholars also imply that we amend the way we conceive of identities to account for media engagements (radically defined) because media texts are a part of the presentation of our social and cultural selves. Audiences' identities are at least partially constructed by their engagement with media texts. Hall (1996) states that identities in general are about representations; they are questions about how one is represented and how one chooses to represent oneself. The image or portrayal of self that is selected is forged through "interactions, relationships, and influences between individuals and institutions" such as the media (Means Coleman 2002, 7). As Franz Fanon states, "There is a constellation of postulates, a series of propositions that slowly and subtly—with the help of books, newspapers, schools and their texts, advertisements, films, radio—work their way into one's mind" (1967, 152), shaping how one views and constructs self in society.

Chris Barker (1997) has also demonstrated that social agents receive multiple narratives of self and social knowledge from diverse sites and contexts of interaction in everyday life, including television texts and discussions of those texts within peer groups. The proffered scripts become a part of the "intersubjective" reflexive process of identity formation, used by subjects to create identity makers and boundaries and to revise and rework their subjectivities. In other words, popular culture and media play a key role in the construction of our subjectivities, sensibilities, and ontologies. Taken together, these claims highlight a dialogic relationship between media and self-presentations or performances, illustrating that what one consumes of mediated fare is constitutive of identity, shaping the way we conceive and present our private and public selves.

The dialogic potential of media engagement is illustrated in black Caribbean women's interaction with U.S. and black Caribbean mainstream media. In this section, I highlight the ways in which black Caribbean women engage with media messages and appropriate them in their self-making processes and negotiations of embodied cultural citizenship in the United States.

Oppositional Responses to "Thin Media"

As discussed earlier, the women in the study have no desire to be thin and actively dismiss and contest the normalcy of the thin body on the basis of their racial and cultural identification. Similarly, the respondents' racial and cultural positions help them to challenge the standardization of thinness in mainstream American media. This is reflective of Hall's (1980) conception of oppositional readings of media texts. Specifically, Hall states that mass media proffer messages and identity positions, but where the readers do not identify with the producers or the position of the media, the interpretation of the message is likely to be different from that of the intended messages. For audiences whose social positions put them in direct conflict with the preferred or dominant reading (such as black Caribbean women who value a different beauty system than the thin ideal), they can have an oppositional response to media in which they fully understand the intended messages but disagree with and reject them.

An oppositional reading is often articulated through "talking back" to media (hooks 1989, 5). According to bell hooks, it is essential for subaltern women, women who are marginalized in society, to find their voices, to "speak as . . . equal[s]" (1989, 5) to institutions and persons of authority and to dare to disagree and have an opinion in the face of silencing, subversive forces. This "talking back" necessarily involves challenging the discourses and ideologies that are circulated in society through media. The media are institutions that differentially interpellate and position people in society, establish and maintain hegemonies, and subsequently secure racist and ethnocentric social stratification. Given this potential, it is important for subalterns to find ways to resist these "controlling images" (Collins 1998).

The women in the study exhibit this form of "talking back," which fosters their oppositional responses to American mainstream media. More precisely, the women "talk back" to mediated discourses that exalt the ideology of thinness. Rather than accept the prevalence of the thin ideal in mainstream media as evidence of its normalcy, the women "speak as equals" to the dominant media of the United States, cogently exposing American media's work in manufacturing a thin norm. Ronda says: "If you're heavy like [Monique] and Tacaara [America's next top model], they will Photoshop you. You might be pretty in the face, but if you are big, they will Photoshop you. They Photoshop Beyoncé, and she is not even that big. So from my observation American culture is more so focused on how slim you are. . . . I think that's kind of what Americans go for, but they kind of put on a show with American culture because what they present in the media are people who are skinny, but most of them are getting surgery." Ronda "calls out" media, highlighting their thinning practices and questioning their construction of "reality." Similarly, Sue says, "This country is all hyped about exercise, but there's a lot a big people around us, so what's up with the exercise? And [it's] all because of what you see on TV." Like her counterpart, Sue thinks television propels contemporary obsession with body sculpting and thinness, manufacturing an esteem of the thin silhouette that she feels is impractical and unrealistic, disconnected from the bodies of real women in society (evidenced by the number of real women in society who are not able to attain it).

The women's own conception of racialized beauty also prompts them to ridicule and criticize black women in the media who they believe try to approximate the "white" body. One respondent, Shera, comments that she and her friends often joke about wanting to meet some of these black television women so that they can feed them and "put some meat on their bones." Several of the respondents also express disappointment with black celebrities, such as singer Jennifer Hudson and talk-show hosts Star Jones and Oprah, who they believe lose weight to approximate mainstream standards. They agree that these women needed to get healthy, but they believe that their weight loss is not reflective to self-empowerment; it is excessive and is directly related to wanting to be more "normal" and pleasing to mainstream (white) audiences. The women's recognition and critique of television's hegemonic work of constructing the norm of thinness, their "talking back," extenuates (even if it does not eliminate) the power of the mediated discourses of thinness to position them negatively in U.S. society.

The women also deploy their personal sense of respectability and style in clothing to undermine the validity and acceptability of thin black and white women in the media. As discussed earlier, self-presentation has a very significant place in the body politics of both first- and second-generation black Caribbean immigrant women: the latter value style, particularly in regards to reflecting "first world" trends and vogues, and the former emphasize respectability as reflected through dress. The women in both generations mobilize these politics of dress to "talk back" to women in the media. They criticize the clothing choices of television characters, stating that their attire is too scant or that the clothing style being worn just does not "look right" on their bodies. For example, Ronda admits that she is more concerned with what television personalities are wearing than with their actual bodies. She says, "I just think about the way a person carries [herself]. You can be flat and you can dress like a skank, and I am going to make a judgment about you. But if you're flat, I'm not going to be like, 'Oh, you're flat.' I don't care." Above body size and shape, what is most important for her are decency and propriety in dress.

Many of the women (particularly in the first generation) also decry television's objectification of women's bodies and its privilege of the physical body over other attributes; they are concerned with this medium's tendency to reduce and confine the definition of femininity to physical characteristics and ultimately dehumanize women. They believe there is undue emphasis on body aesthetics in general, to the neglect of moralistic attributes, such as resilience, perseverance, self-betterment, and self-confidence. Similar to the women in the studies of Lisa Rubin, Mako Fitts, and Anne Becker (2003) and Erynn Casanova (2004), the current participants perceive such inner traits as important elements of women's beauty, the lack of which could detract from even the most physically beautiful women. For example, Natalie passionately expresses her main concern with television's emphasis on physical beauty: "Regardless of what you think, it does put the message in somebody else's head that it's all about what I see. There's more to you than that . . . but [television] make[s] it so much of a focus that it's all about your breast size or your butt size, and it's not so, cause you could be a beautiful person on the outside, and your personality is nasty." Natalie fears that television's failure to promote good character will give young girls and other women false messages and encourage them to strive for the right physique rather than a wholesome character.

Collectively, the women criticize American mainstream mediated images of thinness as unrealistic, vulgar, and shallow and frame them in a manner that allows them to challenge their primacy and validity. Not surprisingly, this evaluation is facilitated by their body politics. Specifically, the women's critique and undermining of the thin regime is directly linked to their "romance" with voluptuousness and endorsement of the thick black female body, which locates them outside dominant American body politics. Claiming a black Caribbean identity, they value a thick body and thus respond oppositionally to thin-promoting discourses.

However, foregrounding the image of the voluptuous black woman in their "talking back" indicates their partial acquiescence to the beauty discourses prevalent in American media. The "thick black woman" ideology is ubiquitous in American mainstream media. These mediated discourses normalize the voluptuous body for black women and cultivate the idea that black women should be big. Indeed, the women admit that they are constantly given the message through media that as black women, they are expected to be thick. In other words, the media help to construct and reinforce the ideology of the "thick black woman" that the women uphold; it is a part of the beauty hegemony of the United States. Using the thick black female body to set themselves apart from thinness and whiteness is thus indicative of the participants' complicity with this part of the thin regime, their partial acceptance of and dominant response to the beauty-society discourses prevalent in American media.

Negotiated Responses to American Media
While the women take an oppositional stance to American media messages that promote the thin aesthetic, they still have to contend with media discourses that construct black women's bodies as thick and ugly and promote their marginalization. To negotiate the negative physical capital and double consciousness fostered by this negative discourse of voluptuousness, the women appropriate other mainstream discourses about the body in the media. In other words, while they outright reject some dominant American media messages regarding thinness, they appropriate others and use them for their benefit. So American media discourses, in spite of serving the beauty hegemony of thinness, help the women in the construction of their embodied cultural citizenship.

This mode of engagement with dominant media texts reflects Hall's negotiated reading, in which readers partly share the text's code and broadly accept the intended message, but modifies the message in a way that reflects their own position, experiences, and interests. The women in the study engage in this form of interpretation; they appropriate discourses, modes of presentations, and beauty tips from the very media that marginalize them. They use this information to negotiate and circumvent body politics and practices that limit their social and economic mobility in the United States.

For instance, both generations' discussion and practice of performativity and mimicry recuperate contemporary obsessions with individualism and self-presentation in the American media. As discussed in previous sections, black Caribbean women in the United States employ dress to perform respectability and Americanness and to ultimately contest the privilege given to thinness in dominant American society. Much of their performance is informed by American television programs that are structured around image improvement. These shows are replete with ideas and suggestions about how to create more aesthetically pleasing and thus more competent femininity through consumerism (Sender 2006; Wood and Skeggs 2004, 203). They present makeup, clothing, beauty products, and cosmetic procedures that can accentuate or hide parts of the body and create the illusion of having the acceptable body. Personal makeover reality shows, which many of the women watch, are the epitome of this trend. Such makeover programs are usually predicated on the humiliation and then deliverance of participants by experts who transform the outmoded, plain, and unattractive into works of beauty (Philips 2005).

These shows also allow audiences to internalize the cosmetic gaze (Wegenstein 2012) by helping them to envision the virtual, mediated bodies of reality stars as their own bodies and highlighting the personal and economic capital that can be gained from changing their bodies into their better selves. Some of these shows deal with acquiring and sculpting the ideal, thin body through dieting, exercise, and even plastic surgery. In others, taste experts, rather than sculpting the bodies of the participants, highlight the clothing that is unacceptable for their particular body types and what should be bought to "make the best" of what they have. Both types of programs depict cosmetic makeovers as the revealing of some "true self" through clothing and/or surgery and are designed to allow one's youthful, or professional, or romantic self to be evident through outward appearance and attire.

As evidence of their negotiated approach to American media, the women seem to accept and focus on the aspect of the self-improvement ideology that is most applicable and relevant to them: dress. They do not appropriate the explicit and implicit rhetoric of thinness that is embedded in notions of self-betterment but rather take up discourses related to "fixing up" themselves and projecting and maintaining a good public image. So while the self-improvement discourses are meant to position voluptuous black Caribbean women as "other" in American society (as always in need of change and never good enough), the women reinterpret them to their own ends and strategically employ them in their creation of embodied cultural citizenship.

The first-generation women appropriate a pervasive self-improvement ideology disseminated by television, which presents clothing (self-presentation) as a means to make any body better (that is, thin). However, they use these self-improvement discourses and counsels to sculpt and perform the accepted body of the Caribbean. The ideas and tips presented in mainstream self-improvement shows are generally intended to help women who do not have the requisite thin body to create the illusion of this silhouette and include advice on issues such as how to make legs, thighs, and waists appear smaller and how to conceal stomachs and buttocks that are deemed too big. The women appropriate these discourses for their own interests. Indeed, they learn from mainstream media how to use dress and clothing in the service of creating the illusion of a voluptuous, "not too big, not too small" body. Recall, for example, Natalie, who wore padded bras and other clothing that would augment her small frame, and Sue, who speaks about wearing minimizers to give the illusion of smaller breasts (correcting the part of her body that violates the "Coca-Cola bottle" shape). She also says: "There are clothes that you put on that even though you're big, [they] make you look smaller. . . . By watching *Oprah*, I've learnt if you wear certain pants [a] certain way, it looks like you don't have a stomach." In this way, then, the dominant American media and popular American culture in general help the women to perform the ideal body of the Caribbean. The women reinterpret self-improvement discourses and the cosmetic gaze that is trained to promote thinness to create flat stomachs and bigger buttocks and to essentially enact the voluptuous figure.

Mainstream American media is also instrumental in the second-generation women's mimicry of Americanness. As discussed in chapter 3, these women actively pursue mainstream American modes of self-presentation; they choose to dress and present their bodies according to

American and European standards, and the adornment of their bodies—
their hairstyles, outfits, shoes, piercings, and accessories—reflect the dominant trends in the United States, specifically those circulating in New
York City. These women get inspiration and ideas for Western outfits
from American media. They do not care for the thin bodies presented
but instead interact with media with a keen eye on what the women are
wearing. From U.S. media they get ideas about color blocking (putting
together seemingly uncomplementary colors), trendy styles, possible
hairstyles, and combining accessories. Karrie, who frequently reads *Essence* and *Cosmopolitan* magazines, says: "When you look through those
[magazines], it'll talk about what nail polish to wear with certain outfits
and what complements what best and stuff like that. So yeah! They talk
about makeup. Learn how to do contouring." Brenda also uses mainstream
magazines to get tips about how to style her body. She says, "*Seventeen*
magazine will tell you what kind of body shape you have and give you
tips like if you have a pear-shaped body, and I am like, 'This is like me! I
should wear that.'" Tony and Veniece similarly use magazines and Tumblr
to look at outfits.

Thus American media (those that target both black and white communities) provide the tools for the women to mimic Western modes of
dress and style and facilitate their acceptance and entrance into spaces that
would have otherwise been closed to them because of the shape and size
of their bodies; these media allow the second-generation women to align
themselves with American fashion and perform and mimic Americanness,
to negotiate oppressive regimes of body politics, and ultimately to insert
themselves into the dominant global economy. In their efforts to cultivate
and promote the image of the acceptable American female citizen, mainstream media supply information that allows subalterns, "noncitizens"
such as black Caribbean women, to put on the trappings of a "legitimate"
citizen and circumvent the low status created by their engagement with
the voluptuous aesthetic. They may not have the accepted thin bodies,
but they dress and care for their bodies as those of the mainstream and
so negotiate their marginalized position in the United States.

Clearly, American media are implicated in the embodied cultural citizenship that the participants develop. Through dominant American mediated discourses, then, the women's bodies are simultaneously condemned and redeemed. They create a negative affect in the women regarding their thick body politics, but they also (unintentionally) offer recommendations and products that the women employ to approximate the voluptuous ideal and to drape the voluptuous black body in American style. In both instances, mainstream media facilitate performances that allow black Caribbean women to gain physical capital in both black Caribbean communities and the mainstream United States. Therefore, rather than engendering the acceptance of their voluptuous bodies as monstrous and valueless, American media texts (unwittingly) give the women ways to endure in the United States while maintaining the thick ideal.

The women's negotiated response to self-improvement media facilitates their cultural and personal empowerment, but by applying these discourses to practices that uphold hegemonic body politics, it also helps to reinforce their marginalized place in the United States. For instance, while helping the women (particularly those of the first generation) to achieve the illusion of voluptuousness, dominant American media also help them maintain the body that contributes to their marginalized position in U.S. society. So while the act of reinterpreting and reframing media texts is indicative of personal agency, it is also important to interrogate how and to what end the appropriated discourses are being used, given that they may be employed (consciously or unconsciously) to underscore existing hegemonies.

Furthermore, these body-improvement media do reinforce oppressive self-monitoring habits. They cultivate the practice of continuous physical enhancements and upgrading, which requires the women to objectify their bodies and internalize surveillance mechanisms. Neither the women of the first generation nor those of the second are strangers to this policing, for they are constantly scrutinized by their diasporic communities and families and have developed their own system of self-monitoring in regard to maintaining a voluptuous figure and wearing appropriate dress.

These body-improvement media further incite this policing by promoting continuous attention to their body size as well as self-presentation. Janet suggests that these media compel vigilance over their bodies by supplying a plethora of cautionary tales in the form of makeover stories, particularly in regard to self-presentation. She says: "What really motivate me is when I watch . . . [shows] where the people [do not take care of themselves] and somebody have to send in their names . . . and just a shampoo and a cut and some rinse, a lipstick or something make such a difference. And I'm saying, 'So why did somebody have to tell them to do this,' you know? They see themselves looking older than their years [and they don't do anything about it]."

Wegenstein (2012) suggests that programs that depict "the before" stories and stories of failed makeover are just as important as the successful makeovers themselves, as they help to mark the boundaries of acceptability, training the cosmetic gaze to identify what is good and what is horrific in personal presentations. Janet's statement indicates the success of such narratives because through these shows, she has learned that women need to be more watchful of their own bodies; she suggests that media remind her never to allow herself to become so unaware of her body that others have to give her a makeover. The televised humiliation of others becomes a warning to be vigilant of her image, placing pressure on her to always police her body.

Finally, it is worth repeating that the women's emphasis on self-presentation echoes the capitalistic consumerism that pervades American media. The women's performance of the ideal black Caribbean body and mimicry of Eurocentric styles is predicated on consumption. It entails the purchase and acquisition of clothes, accessories, and services and in that way reflects this U.S. culture-ideology. Therefore, the embodied cultural citizenship that American media facilitate is embedded within and enacted through capitalistic ideals. It enables negotiations of the imperialistic body politics that the women encounter in their diasporic space, but these negotiations are individualistic and personal (articulated by and through individual acts) and reinforce the profit motives of major multinational corporations. These women appropriate discourses of self-presentation and consumerism to circumvent and evade subjugation in their diasporic space, but by doing so, they concurrently reinscribe the structures and ideologies that seek to exploit them.

Caribbean Media and Embodied Cultural Citizenship
Interestingly, in spite of their presentation of an alternative beauty system (and the potential for negotiation and opposition of the U.S. hegemony that they facilitate), Caribbean media are relatively absent in the women's construction of embodied cultural citizenship in the United States. While American media play a major role in the first- and second-generation women's negotiation of body politics and negative physical capital, the women do not deploy black Caribbean media in this manner at all. None of the women employ them for suggestions about self-presentation in the United States or for help with other "creative revelation" actions to challenge negative physical capital. For them, black Caribbean media may be great for creating and maintaining connections to the cultures of the Caribbean but are not useful for ideas about negotiating hegemonies of the United States. In this sense, then, they have an oppositional response to Caribbean media; they dismiss and reject them as legitimate sources of help in the U.S. diaspora.

There is one main reason for this relative absence of black Caribbean media in the women's construction of embodied cultural citizenship. Many of the women dismiss media oriented toward the black Caribbean diaspora as being ill equipped to deal with issues related to overcoming or negotiating colonial body politics in the American context. As discussed earlier, the women in the second generation perceive black Caribbean self-presentation and style as inexpensive, unoriginal, unmodern, and ultimately incongruous with the image they want to project in the United States. Accordingly, they also view black Caribbean media and the images they project as subpar. Tamara summarizes the general sentiments of the women: "I don't mean to sound bad, but I don't really think I would go on any [Jamaican] website to look for fashion tips, unless I'm doing research on Jamaica. They usually get fashion tips from us!" Handa also says: "I think they are inferior." In other words, media from the Caribbean may be useful for presenting information about the countries of the Caribbean, but their dependency on U.S. media and their inferior production and thematic values make them ineffectual in the context of the United States; these media are not perceived as sophisticated enough to guide these black Caribbean immigrant women through their diasporic space in New York City.

5 EMBODYING DIASPORA
Centering Thick Bodies in Black Women's Diasporic Experiences

In the United States, black women from the English-speaking Caribbean exist within the intersecting regimes of race, class, gender, and coloniality. A pervasive strategy of modern global imperialism, coloniality is a legacy of colonialism that promotes the continued use of race to codify the difference between the colonizer and the colonized (employer and employee, ruler and ruled) in postcolonial states and to undergird labor relations in the modern global economy. Ultimately, coloniality privileges the cultures, societies, and bodies (skin color as well as beauty ideals) of white Europe and marks Africa, African cultures, and blackness in general as inferior (Maldonado-Torres 2007). As women who maintain a "romance" with the "black" aesthetic of voluptuousness in this context, black Caribbean women are marginalized not only on the basis of their race and gender but also because of their body size and shape. In other words, part of the women's diasporic experience is the struggle against body politics, cultural proscriptions, and expectations that dictate how their bodies should look and the differential treatment they should receive in society.

To operate and survive within this milieu of marginalization, black Caribbean women construct *embodied cultural citizenship*, positive body image, self-concept and physical capital amidst the multiple beauty regimes and corresponding obstacles they encounter in their new homes.

This form of citizenship is not conceded but entails negotiating negative physical capital, and the social and psychological challenges created by existing outside American and Caribbean beauty ideologies.

Performativity is central to the women's negotiation of embodied cultural citizenship in the United States. Mimicry, or the reproduction of colonial discourses of body politics and self-presentations, is a significant part of these corporeal negotiations, making them not completely oppositional; it does not allow the women to fully escape or evade the racism and ethnocentrism they face. Nevertheless, these enactments have a subversive potential as they allow black Caribbean women to invert and reframe dominant ideologies about their bodies and challenge negative physical capital. Using dress and self-presentation, the women create alternative beauty discourses outside the existing thick and thin hegemony and contest dominant conventions that police and restrict their bodies. So while they adopt American standards and advice about fashion and dress, by doing so with their nonmainstream bodies, they also challenge existing standards of beauty and insert themselves in the dominant global economy. Therefore, through performance and mimicry, the bodies of black Caribbean women become "third spaces" that reinterpret and re-present the beauty ideals and expectations of their cultural spheres. Additionally, the women decenter the role of outward appearance in their lives through discourses of social position and self-love. They challenge the standards of beauty of both the United States and the black Caribbean that emphasize the visible aspects of a person and define success as the pursuit and maintenance of an ideal body.

What does this suggest? How do the experiences and knowledges produced by these women help us better understand racialized beauty regimes in the United States? First, the women's experiences show us that immigrant black women's success in Western societies varies based on interlocking factors, including race, color, nationality, and body aesthetics. These embodied factors coalesce to influence how their bodies are lived, imagined, and disciplined in their new homes. Reports from the women in the study indicate that their social, economic, and professional marginalization in the United States is exacerbated by their body size. They exist in a beauty hegemony that devalues and punishes their unthin bodies and undermines their positions in the United States; their body type (in relation to their race, socioeconomic status, and nationality) undermines participation in U.S. society. Relatedly, as we examine black Caribbean women's experiences with voluptuous body ideals in the United States, we note that spaces are infused with meanings and shaped by ideas about race, gender, nationality, and bodies. Social and economic spaces, such as workplaces, the fashion industry, and even public streets, are organized by informal norms and policies that reproduce existing power relations. Therefore, relations within these spaces perpetuate inequality. In the case of the women in this study, Eurocentric ideas about their race, gender, nationality, and voluptuous bodies perpetuate their marginalization in mainstream white places.

Existing research on and popular beliefs about beauty ideals and body image indicate that because black women in the United States do not subscribe to the thin ideal of Anglo cultures, they are subsequently relatively resistant to the dominant standards of thinness prevalent in the media and develop a healthier body image than their white peers. However, the experiences of the black immigrant women in this study indicate that dominant images of thinness in U.S. mainstream media help to create an environment that is detrimental to the women's self-concept in the United States. Mainstream media in the United States play a significant role in normalizing, projecting, and disseminating discourses that exoticize, debase, and ostracize the women's bigger bodies; they cultivate the idea that thick (black) female bodies are grotesque.

The display of these ideologies in media does not necessarily alter the women's own desires to pursue and maintain the voluptuous thick ideal but rather allows the women to see themselves through the eyes of Eurocentric society, which creates their distress. These anxieties do not come from their inabilities to attain thin bodies but rather emerge because mediated discourses reveal and confirm the contempt, pity, and condescension with which their bodies are perceived in white American society. In other words, American mainstream media foster their double consciousness. Additionally, popular ideas and beliefs about black women's engagement with the thin hegemony do not reflect the social marginalization that black women experience as they pursue and perform body politics that value a bigger silhouette. As black women who align with a bigger aesthetic, they are marked as incompetent, untidy, and uneducated. In this sense, then, their body type impedes participation in the most lucrative parts of U.S. society; their bodies are negative physical capital that undermine their positions in the United States.

Moreover, research and popular discourses about black women's engagement with the thin hegemony promote the idea that the ideal of voluptuousness in black women is separate from the thin regime of mainstream America and less oppressive. On the contrary, the ideology of the "thick black woman" is embedded in the thin hegemony. Both the thick and the thin regimes have expectations of the big black female body, though to different ends: in the thin, white regime, the idea of the "thick black woman" is used to underscore the abnormality of blackness and the beauty of whiteness and to contain black women to certain prescribed areas of society. In the voluptuous hegemony in black communities, the "thick black woman" is celebrated and venerated as an effort to empower black women and the curves that many have. However, both paradigms of beauty normalize and standardize the voluptuous black body, upholding it as a prerequisite and characteristic of blackness that excludes many. Furthermore, while more explicit in the thin hegemony, the standardization of voluptuousness for black women in both regimes feeds into existing ideologies and practices that were used by imperialists from the sixteenth to the eighteenth centuries. European travel writers in Africa popularized discourses that ascribed big bodies to all black women, a notion that was then used as a signifier of otherness and inferiority and as a marker of their sole utility as laborers and reproducers.

To be clear, my point is not that European colonizers created the voluptuous body type. Furthermore, I am not saying that the celebration of bigger black women is hegemonic, or that women who maintain thick bodies are buying into coloniality. Rather, I argue that the *ideology* that black women *should be* and *are* thick (that is, the standardization of the thick black female body) is a controlling mechanism that has been constructed and used to justify black women's devaluation in modern spaces and thus should not be taken up uncritically. Even though it has been embraced as the standard of feminine beauty for African diaspora societies, to unquestioningly adopt the "thick black woman" ideal is to perpetuate the cycle of social and economic marginalization for black women in the global economy and uphold the colonialist ideas on which it is based. The thin ideal has been widely deconstructed, and many have investigated the ways in which it perpetuates patriarchy (see Bordo 1993, for example). However, an equivalent interrogation of that scale has not been done to investigate the relationship between the voluptuous norm for black (particularly postcolonial) women and racist, imperialist designs.

Second, the women's experiences demonstrate how cultural identity and practices can concurrently exacerbate and ameliorate outsider positions of black immigrant women in the United States and further constrain participation in society. Recent research on embodied stratification (the ways in which bodies are differentially treated in society based on their difference from the established norm) highlights the coconstitutive nature of bodies and inequality (Mason 2013). On the one hand, societies judge raced and gendered bodies, using their difference to legitimize efforts to deny them social, political, and economic mobility. On the other hand, societal factors (such as differing cultural norms) can influence the appearance of those bodies and can exacerbate this difference and perpetuate marginalization. In other words, the norms of subaltern cultural groups related to beauty, diet, and general care and presentation of bodies can cultivate bodies that further reinforce their own unequal treatment in society (Mason 2013). Often these societal beliefs may be the product of acceptance and internalization of dominant ideologies. As Katherine Mason notes, "[As social beliefs] become engrained in early childhood socialization and institutional rules, those beliefs teach members of different groups what sorts of bodies and bodily capacities they should have, thereby eliciting compliance with normative body standards" (2013, 694).

Black immigrant women living in the United States who uphold the voluptuous ideal experience marginalization through a similar process. As seen with the black Caribbean women of this study, they are socialized into the voluptuous ideal by their communities and American and Caribbean media, but by internalizing these expectations (of both their communities and the dominant white society), the women perpetuate their marginalization in the United States. While their cultures embrace the derrière as the standard for black women in the Caribbean, individual black women who embody this characteristic continue to struggle for economic and political equality; they are unable to eschew the social inequalities that accompany having a bigger body in the United States. The cultural and racial expectations of the bodies of black Caribbean immigrant women thus recuperate and perpetuate dialectic ideas about black femininity; on one hand, they provide an alternative to the thin aesthetic promoted in mainstream America, but on the other, they reinscribe neo-imperialistic ideas about the size, shape, and ultimate value of black women's bodies in Western discourse, exacerbating their pathologization in the United States.

In this way, these standards feed into technologies of subjugation and push the women further into the margins of mainstream American social and economic systems; the women (unwittingly) perpetuate the cycle of their social stratification as their embodied cultural identity creates negative physical capital in American society. This marginalization is manifested in the larger global economic system. It is perpetuated in the neoliberal global economy by multibillion-dollar corporations whose profits depend on the maintenance and propagation of this colonial beauty regime; these corporations mobilize these assumptions to sell beauty products, regimens, and clothing and to maintain a system of hierarchy where postcolonial black women (devalued because of their race and body type) are relegated to the lower strata of society.

Nevertheless, subaltern immigrant cultural practices are concurrently beneficial to marginalized groups because they can provide ways to challenge and contest negative social stratification in Western societies. They present alternative discourses and norms that allow disempowered groups to challenge dominant hegemonies, resist subjectifying forces, and construct alternative discourses and ideologies about themselves in the United States. So while the cultural norms of subordinated groups may reinforce their minority status, these customs also facilitate their negotiation of the dominant forces that position them there. In the case of black Caribbean women, their culture and race—the same Caribbean and black heritage that socializes them into a body type that limits their participation in mainstream American society—also help them to negotiate the negative physical capital they face in the United States. Both generations' cultural identity and location as black Caribbean women, which encourages their "romance" with the voluptuous body, allow them to oppose and defy the effects of living in a thin regime. The first-generation women's alignment with Caribbean ideas of respectability permits them to undermine the centrality of physical beauty in Western body politics and challenge their lowered position in American value hierarchies. The flexible identities of the second-generation women, cultivated because of their liminality in the diaspora, foster their movement between American and Caribbean cultures in ways that challenge their exclusion from U.S. society.

Therefore, while it may be tempting to conclude that socialization into the conventions and norms of white American body politics may alleviate or assuage some of the marginalization that subaltern groups face, the experiences of women in my study demonstrate that cultural assimilation may not be the most useful solution. In the first place, acquiescing to dominant systems of body care and presentations in the United States forces immigrant black women to accept body politics, rules, and conventions that inherently exclude them; they would be accepting discourses that are not in their best interest. Natasha Barnes says it best: "The visibility of black women as desirous feminine subjects in historical contexts, such as slavery and colonialism, where such visibility would necessarily bring attenuated pleasures ... should remind us that the politics and performances of female desirability have necessarily uneven emancipatory potential. [There are mixed benefits] of black women's age-old desire to be fully constituted as 'women' in a Western conceptual categorization that has traditionally made women of colour its 'Other'" (2000, 105). For example, the black and mixed-race women who were deemed attractive by European slave owners (and who capitalized on it to escape field labor) were also susceptible to rape and sexual exploitation. Similarly, the female masqueraders of Trinidad Carnival, with their "Rio-styled" outfits (spandex and string bikinis), are, on the one hand, empowered in their *wining* and reveling but, on the other, struggle with sexual harassment within and outside the space of carnival (Barnes 2000).

In other words, even if they embrace the thin aesthetic, as some do, immigrant black women cannot find acceptance in the thin hegemony of the United States because the current system of beauty is also predicated on being white and Western; it is not designed to accommodate them. Moreover, fully relinquishing their cultural practices would result in immigrant black women giving up the very discourses and norms that can be mobilized to contend with and negotiate their lowered status in dominant society. As evidenced by the accounts of the women in the study, their Caribbean identity and the customs, discourses, ideologies, and practices that come with it allow them to build and maintain self-esteem and navigate strictures and ideas in a space that is hostile to them.

Third, the women illustrate how black immigrant women in the United States can and have taken on the entrepreneurial ethos of contemporary neoliberalism to create embodied cultural citizenship. According to Carla Freeman (2014), current entrepreneurialism refers not simply to a mechanism of self-employment but to a more generalized way of being and engaging the world that extends to the invention and reinvention of the self. In an age of neoliberalism, with its "quest for flexibility in the changing marketplace," people at different strata of society take measures to reinvent themselves in ways that make them more suited for enterprise and the market sphere (2014, 1). In this sense, the self is conceived of as an "entrepreneurial 'project' under constant renovation" (2014, 1). The immigrant Caribbean women of this study use discourses and performances to shape and give expressions to their embodied sub-jectivities, renovating themselves in ways that make them more attractive (physically and economically) in the United States. This work that they engage in is not valued in the U.S. capitalistic system because it cannot be commodified, and there is not much measurable evidence that it can be converted into monetary profit. However, their entrepreneurship engen-ders a positive affect that is important to their transition and well-being in the United States; it creates self-worth, confidence, and self-esteem that allow them to negotiate the ideologies and environments that they have to traverse.

Fourth, the women's experiences demonstrate the persistence of gen-dered racial tropes and images around black women's bodies in general. The articulations may vary over time, but black women's bodies have been and continue to be subjected to discursive violence and erasure. Since contact between African populations and Europeans was initiated, black women's bodies have been subjected to visual and rhetorical represen-tations that serve the interests of dominant societies. For example, the carefully constructed pictorial representations of black women in Afri-ca during the colonization period aligned with the missions of imperial expansion by whetting European appetites for unexplored cultures and finding the "primitive savage" (Willis and Williams 2002). Additionally, the image of the "Hottentot Venus" signified the hypersexuality and in-ferior intelligence of black women and justified their exploitation at the hands of Europeans.

The Mammy figure is another controlling image applied to black wom-en in the United States. This epitome of the faithful, obedient domestic servant was created to justify black women's exploitation as domestic slaves and restrict them to domestic service. Mammy's fat body significant-ly contributes to this construction of black femininity as her large body, dark skin, and round facial features cause her to pose no sexual threat to white women (Collins 1991). In other words, her body was used to mark her as unwomanly. In contrast, Jezebel was the "wanton, libidinous black woman whose easy ways excused white men's abuse of their slaves as sexual 'partners' and bearers of mulatto offspring" (Austin 1995, 432). To illustrate her lasciviousness, Jezebel is often presented as having a similar body type to the "Hottentot Venus," with round hips and buttocks. The images of both Mammy and Jezebel were used to justify the economic and sexual exploitation of black female slaves and their more contemporary counterparts.

While the Mammy image has come under much public scrutiny and has fallen out of favor, the "Hottentot Venus"–Jezebel body type continues to circulate in American society (among white as well as black communities). In fact, this image is prolific among black women in contemporary American media. A great example of this can be found in a popular comedy on a major television network about three generations of a black family and how they deal with everyday issues in America. In the pilot episode, the mother character in the show, Rainbow Johnson, defends her blackness by saying, "If I am not black, can somebody please tell my hair and my [buttocks]?" With this one statement, Rainbow reiterates the popular cultural image of black women. She implies that black women's bodies are at least partially defined by the very visible elements of hair texture and, most significantly, a large but proportionate derrière. As such, contemporary black television personalities and characters flaunt their buttocks as a symbol of their sexuality and ultimate black femaleness.

Granted, there are significant differences between Saartjie Baartman and contemporary voluptuous black women on television; many black women on television today are willing and paid participants in the shaping of their image, which raises complex questions about their role in perpetuating racial ideologies. However, these women are still portrayed negatively; women with these bodies in contemporary media are confident, but they connote women of low respectability, hypersexuality, and low intelligence. Their voluptuous bodies have the same significance as they did some two hundred years ago. Contemporary American media thus include cultural symbols that are legacies of the slavery era and colonialism and that reinforce rather than undermine racial ideologies. These negative representations of thick black women on television influence the lives of real black women in the United States: they normalize racial ideologies about black women as lacking self-control and civility and foster environments in which they are marginalized.

I would like to address the recent so-called butt revolution that has been happening in U.S. popular culture. In truth, there has been a general normalization of bigger butts in media over the last few years. For example, television and other mainstream popular culture endorse bigger buttocks, liberally displaying and talking about the buttocks of celebrities and the "butt" augmentations they have done. Popular hip-hop icon Nicki Minaj raps about her "big fat butt" in her 2014 song "Anaconda" from *The Pinkprint* album. Reality star Kim Kardashian and Barbadian American singer Rihanna post pictures of their derrières on Instagram. The lyrics and music video for "Booty" (on the 2014 *A.K.A.* album) by Jennifer Lopez (featuring Iggy Azalea and Nicki Minaj) celebrate and flaunt the big "booty." Such images help to drive a cultural shift in the perception of big buttocks and reflect and fuel a growing trend of "butt augmentations" in the United States. There was a 16 percent increase in the number of "butt implant" procedures performed in the United States in 2013 from the preceding year (Parks 2014). The American Society for Aesthetic Plastic Surgery, a trade group that surveyed 901 doctors, found an even bigger increase in augmentations of the derrière. Silicone implants as well as fat replacement procedures (in which fat is taken from other places on the body and injected into the buttocks) nearly doubled, from 11,527 of both types of procedures in 2013 to 21,446 in 2014 (Connor 2015).

It is important to note that the contemporary obsession with bigger derrières is located within mainstream (middle- and upper-class) white culture. As discussed earlier, black women have been (problematically) socialized to value and pursue a voluptuous body, so this ideal has long been a part of black women's racial and cultural identity. Furthermore, mainstream white American culture has also propagated this ideal for black women. Therefore, the current prominence of bigger buttocks is related not to the thick black female body but rather to the butt on a white female body. Moreover, dominant white societies' fascination with prominent buttocks is not new. For example, the figure of the "Hottentot Venus," with her protruding buttocks, embodied two existing tropes of black femininity in European ideology: the Black Venus, a representation of erotic and sexualized black femininity, and the Savage Hottentot, a "repulsive icon of wildness and monstrosity" (Hobson 2005, 21). Her image thus repelled as well as *attracted* European men and women. According to Janell Hobson (2005), white women of the time donned fashions that created the impression of large buttocks. This illustrates that mainstream white society's interest in the buttocks in the twenty-first century is part of a historical trend of enchantment with this part of black women's bodies.

Furthermore, this normalization of the bigger butt should not be confused with the celebration of the voluptuous black female body. The current fascination with the buttocks does little to alter existing ideas about black women's thick bodies. In fact, the current trend deepens thick black women's indignity. Black women have long been assigned this body type, have embraced this body aesthetic, and have been pathologized for it, but when this body type is modeled on a white body, it is perceived as attractive and beautiful. It reinforces the idea that black women are inherently, irrevocably flawed.

Additionally, by appropriating big buttocks, the recent trend undermines any value or embodied cultural citizenship (such as self-confidence) that black women may have gained from having this physical feature. While problematic, the "thick black woman" image gives black women a body image that is theirs, and that allows them to exist outside the confines of white beauty ideals. By including it in mainstream, white beauty discourses, a space that black women can never enter, Western beauty systems co-opt and neutralize the "power" of the "Hottentot Venus." Finally, given the prerequisite of whiteness in being able to participate in this celebration of bigger buttocks (you have to be a white woman), this recent iteration of the obsession with bigger "butts" actually reinforces the marginalization of thick black women. Since black women can never be white, their bigger bodies are perennially excluded from positive readings and acceptance of the voluptuous body. Therefore, while the buttocks have been positively reframed in dominant white beauty discourses, voluptuous black bodies continue to be marginalized in American popular culture. Based on the reports of black Caribbean women in the study, mainstream American media continue to engender a negative affect toward the "thick black woman," making them feel abnormal.

Finally, the women's experiences highlight how assigning voluptuous bodies to black women in general and then marginalizing them for it feeds into the ideology of color blindness. As explained in the text, Eduardo Bonilla-Silva (2006) conceives of the ideology of color blindness as a means to conceal contemporary racial structures and help to underscore white privilege without incriminating whites (Bonilla-Silva 2006). I argue that the "thick black woman" ideology and accompanying cultural representations are frames that help to underscore racial inequality without overtly using race. Assigning voluptuous bodies to black women, in a society that reads those bodies as deviant, provides a way to pathologize black women without using race. This frame can be used to marginalize black women on the basis of their deviant bodies and position black women as peculiar without using race; they can be ostracized in U.S. society on the basis of their nonconformant values and practices, as represented by their body type. In other words, while race is central to their experiences in American society, the emphasis on their bodies allows dominant society to explain their marginalization in nonracial terms; foregrounding their bodies instead of their race is a post–civil rights strategy that fosters their unequal participation and acceptance in American society.

As seen in the reports of the participants, black Caribbean women routinely have their bodies explicitly and implicitly criticized and "othered" in white (middle-class) spaces in the United States. The size and shape of their bodies are openly discussed in a way that would not be appropriate to discuss their race. In the era of color blindness, it is unpopular, uncivil, and unliberal to comment on people's race (in public and mixed company anyway). So while it may be less accepted to blatantly talk about their "otherness" in racial terms (that is, as a function of their skin color), white coworkers and employers liberally discuss the women's bodies, using their

voluptuousness to mark their difference. However, race has not completely disappeared from this discourse of the body. When their bodies are
surveilled as being out of place in this way (and not those of their thin,
white counterparts) and when the comments are centered around the
bigness of the women's thighs and buttocks (widely used markers of black
femininity), then it becomes evident that race, while obscured, is central
to the comments made about their bodies in these spaces.

To be fair, big white women face similar situations in dominant white
spaces in the United States. Fat bodies in public spaces are read as lazy,
incompetent, and weak, and fat women face discrimination and exclusion
from the mainstream, including the job market and the fashion industry
(Murray 2005). Their fate is thus similar to that meted out to thick black
women in white mainstream society. There is an important distinction,
however. The perceived grotesqueness and unacceptability of fat white
bodies in these spaces largely derives from their girth. Fat white bodies
in dominant American society, particularly those of white women, fall
outside the acceptable size for whiteness; they are failed body projects,
as Samantha Murray (2005) says. In other words, their size makes them
offensive. On the other hand, voluptuous black women are marginalized
not because their bodies are out of line with society's requirements but
because *they* are out of place; the combination of their race, gender, and
body type makes them "dirt." For Mary Douglas (2003), dirt is a social
construct; a thing becomes "dirt" when it is out of place, when it disrupts
the order or organization of society. Douglas says there is no such thing
as absolute "dirt"; things (or persons) are classified as such based on the
particular society within which they are located and their perceived dis-
turbance of the space. Marginalizing such disruptions is not perceived as
a negative movement, then, "but a positive effort to organise the environment" (2003, 2).

History reminds us that this is the way voluptuous black women are
perceived. Saartjie Baartman was put on display precisely because she
was perceived as "dirt" in Europe, and she came to signify the societal
disorder of black women with their protruding (and disruptive) thighs

and buttocks. Photographs by Europeans and Americans in the nineteenth and twentieth century continued this trend and further constructed black women as "dirt." By photographing African and American black women in various states of undress, as naked and seminaked specimens of exotic cultures and strange peoples, anthropologists, scientists, and photographers deny these women's humanity and "normality" (Willis and Williams 2002). Black women were also photographed with white women, not only to provide visual contrast, as Deborah Willis and Carla Williams (2002) argue, but also to underscore the deviant sexuality of the white subjects in the pictures. These images were distributed across Europe and America to an eager public with an insatiable appetite for exotic images.

In contemporary discourses, black women continue to be "othered" because of their race, gender, and body type. Their nonthin, black bodies continue to be used as markers of their inherent difference. As the study illustrates, thick black Caribbean women in mainstream white spaces offend the societal order of the United States, which relegates such women to the outskirts of society. They are expected to be big, but their voluptuous bodies are not intended to occupy dominant white spaces; they can be nannies, health-care workers, housekeepers, and other low-paid workers, but they cannot be professionals.

Caribbean Ethnic Media and Cultural Citizenship

One of the issues revealed in this study is the role of Caribbean media in socializing black Caribbean women into the voluptuous ideal and into a body type that exacerbates their marginalization in American society. Popular culture from the Caribbean that the women consume helps to keep them connected to the Caribbean but simultaneously fails to help the women better position themselves in the United States. Furthermore, the women in the study do not deploy black Caribbean media in their construction of embodied cultural citizenship in the United States. None of the women turn to these media for suggestions about self-presentation in American society or for help with other "creative revelation" actions to challenge negative physical capital and body image disturbances.

The participants' rejection of black Caribbean media in their corporeal negotiations is related to their perception of these media as underdeveloped. Additionally, my study of black Caribbean media in the United States (2014) reveals several aspects of this media that could further weaken their ability to empower the black Caribbean community. Take, for example, the Caribbean International Network (CIN), the subject of my study on black Caribbean media. CIN prides itself on being the only television service that specifically targets black Caribbean communities on the East Coast of the United States (though some of its programs may also be accessed online by people outside of this area). Admittedly, CIN is an empowering factor for English-speaking Caribbean immigrants as it fosters a mediated space in which one of their languages and accompanying sensibilities are privileged and celebrated. However, the network simultaneously enacts its own hierarchies and perpetuates the essentialization and commodification of peoples from the region.

First, CIN simplifies and flattens the Caribbean. Despite its claim to Caribbean programming, as suggested by its name, most CIN programming is created by and addresses Jamaicans. The prominence of Jamaican televisual fare on this "Caribbean" network reproduces and sustains the "Jamaican-ization" of the Caribbean so prevalent in the global imagination; it reinforces the idea that there is little distinction among the countries and that the islands embrace a singular belief in the Jamaican mantra of "one love." Rather than helping to problematize and deconstruct this singular image of the English-speaking Caribbean, CIN instead becomes a part of the media that reinforces it. In fact, even as the network attempts to ameliorate the "symbolic annihilation" of black Caribbean people in the United States, it perpetuates its own eradication of the English-speaking Caribbean by focusing almost exclusively on Jamaica.

Another very conspicuous feature of CIN is that its practices reflect a neoliberal economic agenda that prioritizes profit. Economic neoliberalism refers to policies and processes that promote the deregulation and privatization of businesses so as to achieve optimum economic performance and enhance profit-making opportunities (Kotz 2002; McChesney

2001). In the U.S. media industry (and the global media industry at large), this pursuit of profit has led to the relaxation or elimination of barriers to the commercialization of media and the proliferation of concentrated media ownership (McChesney 2001). Highly concentrated, commercialized media have significant cultural and political implications, including compromising the free press necessary to maintain a democracy and undermining citizens' rights of freedom of expression (McChesney 2001). This model of media ownership is also problematic in its commodification of media audiences (Bermejo 2009). According to Dallas Smythe (1977), capitalistic (commercialized) media, with their prioritization of private interests and profit, use their content to manufacture and serve up media audiences to advertising companies. He argues that "the information, entertainment and 'educational' material transmitted to the audience is an inducement (gift, bribe or 'free lunch') to recruit potential members of the audience and to maintain their loyal attention" (1977, 5).

Similar to many other ethnic media in the United States (see, for example, Shi Yu [2009] and Tanikella [2009]), CIN reflects the values of the neoliberal American media. It is a commercial entity that relies on advertisers and sponsors to earn profit. As such, a significant part of its work is to attract potential advertisers, which it does by offering up the large Anglophone Caribbean communities in New York City. The explicit, self-defined purpose of CIN, as presented in its promotional material, is to create a market for companies. Through promises of connecting viewers to their cultural heritage, CIN entices English-speaking Caribbean people on the East Coast of the United States, securing "eye balls," which it then offers to advertisers in exchange for sponsorship. This market imperative of CIN diminishes the network's ability to truly address the diversity of the English-speaking Caribbean and limits its potential to act as a platform for advocacy for the community; CIN has abdicated its role in constructing informed citizens and empowering communities.

In addition to its operational structure, the content of CIN is also problematic. Specifically, it presents programming that underscores the sociolinguistic power structure of Jamaica. All the programs are broadcast in

English that bears the particular phonological characteristics of educated, upper-class, urbanite Jamaicans. The prevalence of this lilt throughout the network underscores long-standing colonial hierarchies. By proffering programming that showcases this signifier of the (white and brown) Jamaican upper classes, CIN perpetuates the class divisions fostered under colonial rule, which continue to plague contemporary black Caribbean societies. These neocolonial discourses constantly remind CIN audiences of their original social positions, making it more difficult for them to shed their pre-premigration positionalities and placing limits on the diasporic subjectivities that people of the English-speaking Caribbean and Jamaicans in particular can imagine and develop in the United States. Therefore, even as it creates a space for the cultural voices of (some) English-speaking Caribbean people, CIN simultaneously reinforces dominant hierarchies, replicating, preserving, and promoting the position of the elites.

Black Caribbean immigrant women's rejection of Caribbean media may be related to this media's tendency to reinscribe the culture of the Caribbean rather than speak to the lives they currently live. Diasporic identities are constructed and exist within liminal third spaces where the values, traditions, and ideologies of both the receiving country and the homeland are negotiated and remade. While not wholly liberating, this space has a subversive potential as it can allow immigrants to rework dominant cultural norms. Ethnic media are instrumental to the construction of this space as they are some of the places that provide the discourses that immigrants may use to construct their subjectivities and sensibilities in their new homes. As Leela Tanikella states, "Media producers are important agents in the production of diasporic communities because they ... reflect locally constructed identities back to the target communities and also represent these identities in the public sphere" (2009, 170). Therefore, media oriented toward black Caribbean immigrants provide the texts, scripts, and discourses that can shape the way they conceive of and present themselves in the United States.

However, by circulating the hierarchies and ideologies of the Caribbean into the diasporic space, black Caribbean media remind their audience in the United States of their premigration positionalities, and "hail" audiences to reproduce them (Althusser 1971). Rather than multiplying their reinvention possibilities (for instance, by being a forum for discussions about community issues or providing information about resources for advancement), black Caribbean media constrict the process by projecting the Caribbean into the United States, placing limits on the diasporic subjectivities that black Caribbean people can imagine and develop in their new home. Current practices of CIN and other commercialized black Caribbean media thus do not promote the welfare of black Caribbean communities in the United States.

In spite of their potential to help black Caribbean women construct discourses and behaviors that can lead to new opportunities for social and economic mobility in their new homes, black Caribbean media function as social control for the homeland, replicating, preserving, and promoting ideologies that are neither relevant nor useful in the diaspora; while the presence of black Caribbean media works to allow the margins to speak back to the center and thus contest existing power structures regulating American spaces, these media do not allow the margins to be remade or reimagined. With these media's perpetuation of colonial and neocolonial hierarchies of the Caribbean and their primary pursuit of profit, it is not surprising that the black Caribbean women of the study do not look to them for discourses, scripts, and practices that can help them negotiate their diasporic space. The women use these media to stay connected to their heritage, so they are a large part of how they are socialized into "romances" with the Caribbean, including their "romance" with voluptuousness, but the women do not find them useful in providing aid to traverse American structures with their voluptuous bodies.

This is not to say that CIN and other media like it should explicitly and positively address the black female body in the United States (though that is also a welcomed option). We can recall that American media do not represent the "thick black woman" in a positive light, but their discourses are mobilized by the women in the study to negotiate the negative affect and consequences related to maintaining a voluptuous aesthetic.

Rather, the important element is diversifying the possibilities presented across the spectrum of the medium. As this study and others have illustrated, audiences do not engage with media in a single moment, nor are they influenced by a single idea or ideology; rather, media engagement is a more holistic experience that draws on multiple texts across multiple media that are mobilized in multiple ways.

In other words, what is essential is not for CIN and other English-speaking Caribbean media to explicitly and exclusively discuss the "thick black woman" but rather to offer a variety of ways or lens across its programming through which black Caribbean women can reimagine themselves in the United States. For example, such media could present empowering, strong (rather than stereotypical) images of the Caribbean and its peoples; they could highlight the diversity of the people, rather than homogenize and simplify the region; they could also specifically address issues that affect the diaspora, not only those that affect the Caribbean. The presentation of all these ideas could give black Caribbean women energizing and inspiring images and discourses that may be used to build their self-esteem, confidence, and courage to challenge existing systems that marginalize their bodies in the United States. Of course, English-speaking Caribbean media cannot control how their images are received and interpreted, nor can they do much about how they are perceived because of their affiliation with the Caribbean, a space that the second-generation women view as backward, conservative, unmodern, and thus irrelevant to their lives in the United States. However, they do control what they present and how they choose to represent the Caribbean.

NOTES

1. The "Thick Black Woman"

1. Given that cultures and the body politics they produce are not constant but continuously shift in relation to social and political ideologies, this reflection should be seen as a snapshot of a particular moment in history, and not as *the* discourse of the body of the English-speaking Caribbean. Moreover, in light of the inextricable relationship between body politics and social markers, including class, it would be problematic to suggest that the description presented here is upheld by all sectors of black Caribbean society or even across Caribbean nations. Therefore, though what I present here would be considered the norm of Jamaica, it should be noted that there are variations based on many factors, including class and nationality.

2. Other images of black womanhood have surfaced throughout the years, the most notable and recognizable being the Mammy figure. The image of the Hottentot Venus is often set against the more palatable image of the loveable Mammy, a domestic woman whose fat body signified asexuality, an overabundance of maternal resources, "an infinite reserve of maternal dedication, suggesting an inability of black women to be oppressed since their supply of strength, love, and other emotional resources can never be depleted," and "the ultimate state of black allegiance to whiteness: the ready availability of nurture despite her own economic oppression effected by those she must serve" (Shaw 2005, 146).

3. See, for example, Renee Botta (2000) and Deborah Schooler, Monique Ward, Ann Merriwether, and Allison Caruthers (2004).

4. The total of 32,878 includes the permanent residency issued to persons from Aruba, Antigua and Barbuda, Barbados, Dominica, Grenada, Guyana, Jamaica, Montserrat, Saint Kitts and Nevis, Saint Lucia, Saint Vincent and the Grenadines, and Trinidad and Tobago. North America refers to Canada, Greenland, Mexico, Saint Pierre and Miquelon, and the United States, as well as countries in the Caribbean and Central American regions.

5. "Going natural" refers to the practice of not chemically treating one's hair.

2. Constructing Diasporic Identity

1. All names of participants are pseudonyms.

2. Here I am distinguishing *nation* (a collective of people claiming a common bond, such as culture) from *state* (a sovereign, political territory).

3. Unrequited Romance

1. Regarding the link between skin color and identity, see, for example, Hunter (2005).

2. See, for example, Hunter (2005).

3. In the black Caribbean, specifically Jamaican, context, "browning" is a colloquial term for a light-skinned black woman. This term is prolific in Jamaican popular culture, particularly dance-hall reggae (see, for example, Hope 2011 and Thame 2011a).

4. See Meeks (2000).

5. This refers to the diet plan that singer Beyoncé Knowles allegedly used to lose weight for the movie *Dreamgirls*. It consists of eating nothing for two weeks, surviving instead on a detox drink made of lemon juice, water, and cayenne pepper. While widely believed to be true, Knowles's use of the diet plan is unconfirmed.

4. Transgressive Discourses

1. While I find Judith Butler's deconstruction of gendered identity useful in articulating the experiences and enactments of black Caribbean diasporic women, I, like many others, do not share her early belief that there is no subject prior to performances.

2. White Plains Road is one of the main thoroughfares in northeastern Bronx and is the center of the black Caribbean community in this borough.

3. These readings will be discussed in more detail later in the chapter.
4. In the period following the Payne Fund studies and Hadley Cantril's study of the "War of the Worlds" broadcast, scholars of mass communications were of the opinion that the mass media were capable of exerting direct, uniform, and powerful influence over the behavior of audience members.

REFERENCES

Acker, Joan, Kate Barry, and Johanna Essveld. 1991. "Objectivity and Truth: Problems in Doing Feminist Research." In *Beyond Methodology: Feminist Scholarship and Lived Research*, edited by Mary M. Fonow and Judith A. Cook, 133–53. Bloomington: Indiana University Press.

Alexander, Simone. 2014. *African Diasporic Women's Narratives: Politics of Resistance, Survival, and Citizenship*. Gainesville: University Press of Florida.

Althusser, Louis. 1971. "Ideology and Ideological State Apparatuses." In *Lenin and Philosophy, and Other Essays*, translated by Ben Brewster, 127–88. London: New Left Books.

Ang, Ien. 1996. *Living Room Wars: Rethinking Media Audiences for a Postmodern World*. London: Routledge.

Anzaldua, Gloria. 1987. *Borderlands/La Frontera: The New Meztiza*. San Francisco: Aunt Lute Books.

Austin, Regina. 1995. "Sapphire Bound!" In *Critical Race Theory: The Key Writings That Firmed the Movement*, edited by Kimberle Crenshaw, Neil Gotanda, Gary Peller, and Kendall Thomas, 426–37. New York: New Press.

Bailey, Marlon. 2013. *Butch Queens Up in Pumps: Gender Performance, and Ballroom Culture in Detroit*. Ann Arbor: University of Michigan Press.

Bakare-Yusuf, Bibi. 2006. "Fabricating Identities: Survival and the Imagination in Jamaican Dancehall Culture." *Fashion Theory: The Journal of Dress, Body and Culture* 10 (4): 461–83.

Banks, Ingrid. 2000. *Hair Matters: Beauty, Power, and Black Women's Consciousness*. New York: New York University Press.

Barker, Chris. 1997. "Television and the Reflexive Project of the Self: Soaps, Teenage Talk and Hybrid Identities." *British Journal of Sociology* 48 (4): 611–28.

Barnes, Natasha. 2000. "Body Talk: Notes on Women and Spectacle in Contemporary Carnival." *Small Axe* 4 (1): 93–105.

Beauboeuf-Lafontant, Tamara. 2009. *Behind the Mask of the Strong Black Woman: Voice and Embodiment of a Costly Performance*. Philadelphia: Temple University Press.

Beckles, Hilary. 1999. *Centering Woman: Gender Discourses in Caribbean Slave Society*. Kingston, Jamaica: Ian Randle.

Ben-Ezer, Gadi. 2002. *The Ethiopian Jewish Exodus: Narratives of the Migration Journey to Israel 1977–1985*. London: Routledge.

Bermejo, Fernando. 2009. "Audience Manufacture in Historical Perspective: From Broadcasting to Google." *New Media Society*, 11 (1–2): 133–54.

Bhabha, Homi. 1994. *The Location of Culture*. New York: Routledge.

Bogues, Anthony. 2002. "Politics, Nation and Postcolony: Caribbean Inflections." *Smallaxe* 6 (1): 1–30.

Bonilla-Silva, Eduardo. 2006. *Racism without Racists: Color-Blind Racism and the Persistence of Racial Inequality in America*. Lanham MD: Rowman & Littlefield.

Bordo, Susan. 1993. *Unbearable Weight: Feminism, Western Culture, and the Body*. Berkeley: University of California Press.

Botta, Renee. 2000. "The Mirror Image of Television: A Comparison of Black and White Adolescents' Body Image." *Journal of Communication* 50 (3): 144–59.

Bourdieu, Pierre. 1984. *Distinction: A Social Critique of the Judgment of Taste*. Translated by Richard Nice. Cambridge MA: Harvard University Press.

———. 1986. "The Forms of Capital." In *Handbook of Theory and Research for the Sociology of Education*, edited by John Richardson, 241–58. New York: Greenwood.

Bova, Breda. 2000. "Mentoring Revisited: The Black Woman's Experience." *Mentoring and Tutoring* 8 (1): 5–16.

Boyce-Davies, Carol. 2010. "Black/Female/Bodies Carnivalized." In *Black Venus 2010: They Called Her "Hottentot,"* edited by Deborah Willis, 186–98. Philadelphia: Temple University Press.

Brah, Avtar. 2001. "Difference, Diversity, Differentiation." In *Feminism and "Race,"* edited by Kum-Kum Bhavnani, 456–78. New York: Oxford University Press.

———. 2003. "Diaspora, Border, and Transnational Identity." In *Feminist Postcolonial Theory: A Reader,* edited by Reina Lewis and Sara Mills, 613–34. New York: Routledge.

Brown-Glaude, Winnifred. 2011. *Higglers in Kingston: Women's Informal Work in Jamaica.* Nashville TN: Vanderbilt University Press.

Bryce-Laporte, Roy. 1972. "Black Immigrants: The Experience of Invisibility and Inequality." *Journal of Black Studies* 3 (1): 20–56.

———. 1987. "New York City and the New Caribbean Immigration: A Contextual Statement." In *Caribbean Life in New York City: Sociocultural Dimensions,* edited by Constance Sutton and Elsa Chaney, 51–69. New York: Center for Migration Studies.

Burton, Richard. 1997. *Afro-Creole: Power, Opposition and Play in the Caribbean.* Ithaca NY: Cornell University Press.

Butler, Judith. 1992. "'The Body You Want': Liz Kotz Interviews Judith Butler." *Art Forum* 31 (3): 82–89.

———. 1999. *Gender Trouble: Feminism and the Subversion of Identity.* New York: Routledge.

Butterfield, Sherry-Ann. 2004. "'We're Just Black': The Racial and Ethnic Identities of Second-Generation West Indians in New York." In *Becoming New Yorkers: Ethnographies of the New Second Generation,* edited by Philip Kasinitz, John Mollenkopf, and Mary Waters, 288–312. New York: Russell Sage Foundation.

Casanova, Erynn. 2004. "'No Ugly Women': Concepts of Race and Beauty among Adolescent Women in Ecuador." *Gender and Society* 18 (3): 287–308.

Center for Immigration Studies. 1995. "Three Decades of Mass Immigration: The Legacy of the 1965 Immigration Act." July 9. http://cis.org/1965Immigration Act-MassImmigration.

Chaney, Elsa. 1987. "The Context of Caribbean Migration." In *Caribbean Life in New York City: Sociocultural Dimensions,* edited by Constance Sutton and Elsa Chaney, 3–14. New York: Center for Migration Studies.

Charles, Christopher. 2010. "Skin Bleaching in Jamaica: Self Esteem, Racial Self Esteem, and Black Identity Transactions." *Caribbean Journal of Psychology* 3 (1): 25–39.

———. 2011. "Skin Bleaching and the Prestige Complexion of Sexual Attraction." *Sexuality and Culture* 15 (4): 375–90.

Chow, Rey. 2013. "The Provocation of *Dim Sum*; or, Making Diaspora Visible on Film." In *Diasporic Chineseness after the Rise of China: Communities and Cultural Production*, edited by Julia Kuehn, Kam Louie, and David Pomfret, 100–110. Vancouver: University of British Columbia Press.

Clifford, James. 1994. "Diaspora." *Cultural Anthropology* 9 (3): 302–38.

Collins, Patricia H. 1991. *Black Feminist Thought*. London: Routledge.

———. 1998. *Fighting Words: Black Women and the Search for Justice*. Minneapolis: University of Minnesota Press.

Connor, Tracy. 2015. "Butt Augmentation, Labiaplasty on the Rise, Plastic Surgeons Say." NBC *News*, March 2. http://www.nbcnews.com/news/us-news/butt-augmentation-labiaplasty-rise-plastic-surgeons-say-n312996.

Cooper, Carolyn. 1995. *Noises in the Blood: Orality, Gender and the "Vulgar" Body of Jamaican Popular Culture*. Durham NC: Duke University Press.

———. 2004. *Soundclash: Jamaican Dancehall Culture At-Large*. Palgrave Macmillan.

Craig, Maxine. 2002. *Ain't I A Beauty Queen? Black Women, Beauty, and the Politics of Race*. Oxford: Oxford University Press.

Darling-Wolf, Fabienne. 2004. "Sites of Attractiveness: Japanese Women and Westernized Representations of Feminine Beauty." *Critical Studies in Mass Communication* 21 (4): 325–45.

Davison, W. Phillips. 1983. "The Third Person Effect in Communication." *Public Opinion Quarterly* 47 (1): 1–15.

Douglas, Mary. 2003. *Purity and Danger: An Analysis of Concepts of Pollution and Taboo*. London: Routledge.

Du Bois, Christine. 2004. *Images of West Indians in the Mass Media: The Struggle for a Positive Ethnic Reputation*. New York: LFB Scholarly Publishing.

Du Bois, W. E. B. 1903. *The Souls of Black Folk: Essays and Sketches*. Cambridge MA: University Press John Wilson and Son.

Edmondson, Belinda, ed. 1999. *Caribbean Romances: The Politics of Regional Representation*. Charlottesville: University of Virginia Press.

Espiritu, Yen L. 2001. "'We Don't Sleep Around Like White Girls Do': Family, Culture, and Gender in Filipina American Lives." *Signs* 26 (2): 415–40.

Fanon, Franz. 1967. *Black Skin, White Masks*. New York: Grove Press.

Foner, Nancy. 1986. "Sex Roles and Sensibilities: Jamaican Women in New York and London." In *International Migration: The Female Experience,* edited by Rita Simon and Caroline Brettell, 133–51. Totowa NJ: Rowman & Allenheld.

———. 1997. "The Immigrant Family: Cultural Legacies and Cultural Changes." *International Migration Review* 31 (4): 961–74.

———. 1998. "West Indian Identity in the Diaspora: Comparative and Historical Perspectives." *Latin American Perspectives* 25 (3): 173–88.

———. 2001. "Introduction: West Indian Migration to New York; An Overview." In *Islands in the City: West Indian Migration to New York,* edited by Nancy Foner, 1–22. Los Angeles: University of California Press.

Freeman, Carla. 2014. *Entrepreneurial Selves: Neoliberal Respectability and the Making of a Caribbean Middle Class.* Durham NC: Duke University Press.

Gentles-Peart, Kamille. 2009a. "Adapting America: West Indian Women's Cultural Adaption of the American Diasporic Space." In *The Theme of Cultural Adaptation in American History, Literature, and Film: Cases When the Discourse Changed,* edited by Lawrence Raw, Tanfer Tunc, and Gulriz Buken, 297–313. Lewiston NY: Edwin Mellen Press.

———. 2009b. "Transnational Television and West Indian Women's Diasporic Identity." In *Global Cultures,* edited by Frank Salamone, 111–30. Newcastle upon Tyne, England: Cambridge Scholars Press.

———. 2014. "'Fiwi TV': Ethnic Media and the West Indian Diaspora." *International Journal of Cultural Studies* 17 (6): 603–17.

Gentles-Peart, Kamille, and Maurice L. Hall. 2012. Introduction to *Re-Constructing Place and Space: Media, Culture, Discourse and the Constitution of Caribbean Diasporas,* edited by Kamille Gentles-Peart and Maurice L. Hall, 1–14. Newcastle upon Tyne, England: Cambridge Scholars.

Gerbner, George, and Larry Gross. 1976. "Living with Television: The Violence Profile." *Journal of Communication* 26 (2): 173–99.

Glazer, Nathan, and Daniel Patrick Moynihan. 1963. *Beyond the Melting Pot: The Negroes, Puerto Ricans, Jews, Italians, and Irish of New York City.* 2nd ed. Cambridge MA: MIT Press.

Good Hair: Sit Back and Relax. 2009. Directed by Jeff Stilson. Produced by Chris Rock. HBO Films. DVD.

Gorelick, Sherry. 2003. "Contradictions of Feminist Methodology." *Gender and Society* 5 (4): 459–77.

Hall, Stuart. 1980. "Encoding/Decoding." In *Culture, Media, Language: Working Papers in Cultural Studies 1972–79*, edited by Stuart Hall, Dorothy Hobson, Andrew Lowe, and Paul Willis, 128–38. London: Methuen.

———. 1990. "Cultural Identity and Diaspora." In *Identity: Community, Culture, Difference*, edited by Jonathan Rutherford, 222–38. London: Lawrence & Wishart.

———. 1996. "Introduction: Who Needs 'Identity'? In *Questions of Cultural Identity*, edited by Stuart Hall and Paul Du Gay, 1–17. Thousand Oaks CA: Sage.

Harley, D. A. 2008. "Maids of Academe: African American Women Faculty at Predominately White Institutions." *Journal of African American Studies* 12:19–36.

Harris-Lacewell, Melissa. 2001. "No Place to Rest: African American Political Attitudes and the Myth of Black Women's Strength." *Women and Politics* 23 (3): 1–33.

Henderson, Tammy, Andrea Hunter, and Gladys Hildreth. 2010. "Outsiders within the Academy: Strategies for Resistance and Mentoring African American Women." *Michigan Family Review* 14 (1): 28–41.

Henry, Paget. 2002. "On The Revisiting of Caribbean Fanonism." *Social and Economic Studies* 51 (2): 195–98.

Herndon, April Michelle. 2005. "Collateral Damage from Friendly Fire? Race, Nation, Class and the 'War against Obesity.'" *Social Semiotics* 15 (2): 127–41.

Hintzen, Percy. 2001. *West Indians in the West: Self-Representations in an Immigrant Community*. New York: New York University Press.

Ho, Christine. 1999. "Caribbean Transnationalism as a Gendered Process." *Latin American Perspectives* 26 (5): 34–54.

Hobson, Janell. 2003. "The 'Batty' Politic: Toward an Aesthetics of the Black Female Body." *Hypatia* 18 (4): 87–105.

———. 2005. *Venus in the Dark: Blackness and Beauty in Popular Culture*. London: Routledge.

hooks, bell. 1989. *Talking Back: Thinking Feminist, Thinking Black*. Boston: South End Press.

Hope, Donna. 2011. "From *Browning* to *Cake Soap*: Popular Debates on Skin Bleaching in the Jamaican Dancehall." *Journal of Pan African Studies* 4 (4): 165–94.

Hunter, Margaret. 2005. *Race, Gender and the Politics of Skin Tone*. New York: Routledge.

Johnston, Josée, and Judith Taylor. 2008. "Feminist Consumerism and Fat Activists: A Comparative Study of Grassroots Activism and the Dove Real Beauty Campaign." *Signs* 33 (4): 941–66.

Jones, Charisse, and Kumea Shorter-Gooden. 2004. *Shifting: The Double Lives of Black Women in America*. New York: Perennial.

Justus, Joyce. 1983. "West Indians in Los Angeles: Community and Identity." In *Caribbean Immigration to the United States*, edited by Roy Bryce-Laporte and Delores Mortimer, 130–48. Washington DC: Research Institute on Immigration and Ethnic Studies, Smithsonian Institution.

Kotz, David. 2002. "Globalization and Neoliberalism." *Rethinking Marxism* 14 (2): 64–79.

LaBennett, Oneka. 2011. *She's Mad Real: Popular Culture and West Indian Girls in Brooklyn*. New York: New York University Press.

Lau, Kimberly. 2011. *Body Language: Sisters in Shape, Black Women's Fitness, and Feminist Identity Politics*. Philadelphia: Temple University Press.

Lorde, Audre. 2007. "The Master's Tools Will Never Dismantle the Master's House." In *Sister Outsider: Essays and Speeches*, edited by Audre Lorde, 110–14. Berkeley CA: Crossing Press.

Maldonado-Torres, Nelson. 2007. "On the Coloniality of Being: Contributions to the Development of a Concept." *Cultural Studies* 21 (2–3): 240–70.

Mason, Katherine. 2013. "Social Stratification and the Body: Gender, Race, and Class." *Sociology Compass* 7 (8): 686–98.

McChesney, Robert. 2001. "Global Media, Neoliberalism, and Imperialism." *Monthly Review: An Independent Socialist Magazine*, March. http://monthly review.org/2001/03/01/global-media-neoliberalism-and-imperialism/.

Means Coleman, Robin. 2002. "The Menace II Society Murder Case and the Thug Life: A Reception Study with a Convicted Criminal." In *Say It Loud! African-American Audiences, Media, and Identity*, edited by Robin Means Coleman, 249–85. New York: Routledge.

Meeks, Brian. 2000. *Narratives of Resistance: Jamaica, Trinidad, the Caribbean*. Kingston, Jamaica: University of the West Indies Press.

Miller, Toby. 2006. *Cultural Citizenship: Cosmopolitanism, Consumerism, and Television in a Neoliberal Age*. Philadelphia: Temple University Press.

Minh-Ha, Trinh. 1990. "Not You/Like You." In *Making Face, Making Soul, Haciendo Caras: Creative and Critical Perspectives by Feminists of Color*, edited by Gloria Anzaldua, 371–75. San Francisco: Aunt Lute Books.

Model, Suzanne. 2001. "Where New York's West Indians Work." In *Island in the City: West Indian Migration to New York*, edited by Nancy Foner, 52–80. Los Angeles: University of California Press.

Mohammed, Patricia. 2000. "'But Most of All Mi Love Me Browning': The Emergence in Eighteenth and Nineteenth-Century Jamaica of the Mulatto Woman as the Desired." *Feminist Review* 65:22–48.

Morgan, David. 1997. *Focus Groups as Qualitative Research*. Thousand Oaks CA: Sage.

Morgan, Jennifer. 1997. "'Some Could Suckle over Their Shoulder': Male Travelers, Female Bodies, and the Gendering of Racial Ideology, 1500–1770." *William and Mary Quarterly* 54 (1): 167–92.

Morley, David, and Kevin Robins. 1995. *Spaces of Identity: Global Media, Electronic Landscapes and Cultural Boundaries*. London: Routledge.

Mose Brown, Tamara. 2011. *Raising Brooklyn: Nannies, Childcare and Caribbeans Creating Community*. New York: New York University Press.

Murray, Samantha. 2005. "(Un/Be)Coming Out? Rethinking Fat Politics." *Social Semiotics* 15 (2): 153–63.

Narayan, Kirin. 2003. "How Native Is a 'Native' Anthropologist?" In *Feminist Postcolonial Theory: A Reader*, edited by Reina Lewis and Sara Mills, 285–305. New York: Routledge.

New York Department of City Planning. 2013. "Population Facts." http://www.nyc.gov/html/dcp/html/census/census_2010.shtml.

Nichols, Grace. 1984. *The Fat Black Woman's Poems*. London: Virago Press.

Omi, Michael, and Howard Winant. 2014. *Racial Formation in the United States: From the 1960s to the 1990s*. New York: Routledge.

Ong, Aihwa. 1996. "Cultural Citizenship as Subject-Making: Immigrants Negotiate Racial and Cultural Boundaries in the United States." *Current Anthropology* 37 (5): 737–62.

———. 1999. *Flexible Citizenship: The Cultural Logic of Transnationality*. Durham NC: Duke University Press.

Parks, Chanel. 2014. "Butt Implants Are on the Rise." *Huffington Post*, February 26. http://www.huffingtonpost.com/2014/02/26/butt-implants-procedures-report_n_4858726.html.

Patton, Tracy Owens. 2006. "Hey Girl, Am I More Than My Hair? African American Women and Their Struggles with Beauty, Body Image, and Hair." *NWSA Journal* 18 (2): 24–51.

Philips, Deborah. 2005. "Transformation Scenes: The Television Interior Makeover." *International Journal of Cultural Studies* 8 (2): 213–29.

Phoenix, Ann. 2001. "Practicing Feminist Research: The Intersection of Gender and 'Race' in the Research Process." In *Feminism and "Race,"* edited by Kum-Kum Bhavnani, 203–19. New York: Oxford University Press.

Portes, Alejandro, and Ramon Grosfoguel. 1994. "Caribbean Diasporas: Migration and Ethnic Communities." *Annals of the American Academy of Political and Social Science* 533 (1): 48–69.

Rosaldo, Renato. 1997. "Cultural Citizenship, Inequality, and Multiculturalism." In *Latino Cultural Citizenship: Claiming Identity, Space, and Rights*, edited by William Flores and Rina Benmayor, 27–38. Boston: Beacon Press.

Rowe, Rochelle. 2009. "'Glorifying the Jamaican Girl': The 'Ten Types–One People' Beauty Contest, Racialized Femininities, and Jamaican Nationalism." *Radical History Review* 2009 (103): 36–58.

Rubin, Lisa, Mako Fitts, and Anne Becker. 2003. "'Whatever Feels Good in My Soul': Body Ethics and Aesthetics among African American and Latina Women." *Culture, Medicine and Psychiatry* 27 (1): 49–75.

Rytina, Nancy. 2006. "Estimates of Legal Permanent Resident Population and Population Eligible to Naturalize in 2004." Department of Homeland Security, Office of Immigration Statistics. http://www.dhs.gov/xlibrary/assets/statistics/publications/LPRest2004.pdf.

Schooler, Deborah, Monique Ward, Ann Merriwether, and Allison Caruthers. 2004. "Who's That Girl: Television's Role in the Body Image Development of Young White and Black Women." *Psychology of Women Quarterly* 28 (1): 38–47.

Sedgwick, Eve. 1990. *Epistemology of the Closet*. Berkeley: University of California Press.

Sender, Katherine. 2006. "Queens for a Day: *Queer Eye for the Straight Guy* and the Neoliberal Project." *Critical Studies in Media Communication* 23 (2): 131–51.

Sharpe, Jenny. 2002. *Ghosts of Slavery: A Literary Archaeology of Black Women's Lives*. Minneapolis: University of Minnesota Press.

Shaw, Andrea. 2005. "The Other Side of the Looking Glass: The Marginalization of Fatness and Blackness in the Construction of Gender Identity." *Social Semiotics* 15 (2): 143–52.

———. 2006. *The Embodiment of Disobedience: Fat Black Women's Unruly Political Bodies.* Oxford: Lexington Books.

Sheller, Mimi. 2003. *Consuming the Caribbean: From Arawaks to Zombies.* London: Routledge.

Shilling, Chris. 1991. "Educating the Body: Physical Capital and the Production of Social Inequalities." *Sociology* 25 (4): 653–72.

———. 2004. "Physical Capital and Situated Action: A New Direction for Corporeal Sociology." *British Journal of Sociology of Education* 25 (4): 473–87.

———. 2005. *The Body in Culture, Technology and Society.* London: Sage.

———. 2012. *The Body and Social Theory.* London: Sage.

Shi Yu. 2009. "Re-Evaluating the Alternative Role of Ethnic Media in the U.S.: The Case of the Chinese-Language Press and Working-Class Women Readers." *Media, Culture and Society* 31 (4): 597–616.

Sklair, Leslie. 1995. "Social Movements and Global Capitalism." *Sociology* 29 (3): 495–512.

Smythe, D. W. 1977. "Communications: Blindspot of Western Marxism." *Canadian Journal of Political and Social Theory* 1 (3): 1–27.

Spillers, Hortense. 1987. "Mama's Baby, Papa's Maybe: An American Grammar Book." *Diacritics* 17 (2): 64–81.

Spivak, Gayatri. 1988. "Can the Subaltern Speak?" In *Marxism and the Interpretation of Culture,* edited by Cary Nelson and Lawrence Grossberg, 271–313. London: Macmillan.

Stacey, Judith. 1988. "Can There Be a Feminist Ethnography?" *Women's Studies International Forum* 11 (1): 21–27.

Strelitz, Larry. 2004. "Against Cultural Essentialism: Media Reception among South African Youths." *Media, Culture and Society* 26 (5): 625–41.

Sutton, Constance, and Susan R. Makiesky-Barrow. 1987. "Migration and West Indian Racial and Ethnic Consciousness." In *Caribbean Life in New York City: Sociocultural Dimensions,* edited by Constance Sutton and Elsa M. Chaney, 86–107. New York: Center for Migration Studies of New York.

Tanikella Leela. 2009. "Voices from Home and Abroad: New York City's Indo-Caribbean Media." *International Journal of Cultural Studies* 12 (2): 167–85.

Thame, Maziki. 2011a. "Against Black Nationalism: Brown Power in Jamaica in Early Independence (1960–80)." *76 King Street—The Journal of Liberty Hall: The Legacy of Marcus Garvey* 2:7–22.

———. 2011b. "Reading Violence and Postcolonial Decolonization through Fanon: The Case of Jamaica." *Journal of Pan African Studies* 4 (7): 75–93.

———. 2014. "Political Context of Social Movement Activism in Jamaica." Paper presented at the Political Context of Social Movement Activism in Jamaica Seminar, Brown University, Providence RI, June 26.

Thomas, Deborah. 2004. *Modern Blackness: Nationalism, Globalization, and the Politics of Culture in Jamaica.* Durham NC: Duke University Press.

Thompson, Susan. 2014. "Accepting Authoritarianism? Everyday Resistance as Political Consciousness in Post-Genocide Rwanda." In *Civic Agency in Africa: Arts of Resistance in the 21st Century*, edited by Ebenezer Obadare and Wendy Willems, 104–24. New York: James Currey.

Tuchman, Gaye. 1978. "Introduction: The Symbolic Annihilation of Women by the Mass Media." In *Hearth and Home: Images of Women in the Mass Media*, edited by Gaye Tuchman, A. Daniels, and J. Benet, 3–38. Oxford: Oxford University Press.

U.S. Census Bureau. 2010. "Place of Birth for Foreign-Born Population." http://metrolina.org/wp/wp-content/uploads/2012/07/Place-of-Birth-for-Foreign-Born-Population-in-Charlotte.pdf.

U.S. Department of Homeland Security. 2011. "Yearbook of Immigration Statistics: 2011." http://www.dhs.gov/sites/default/files/publications/immigration-statistics/yearbook/2011/ois_yb_2011.pdf.

Vickerman, Milton. 1999. "Representing West Indians in Film: Ciphers, Coons, and Criminals." *Western Journal of Black Studies* 23 (2): 83–96.

Warren, John, and Deanna Fassett. 2011. *Communication: A Critical/Cultural Introduction.* Thousand Oaks CA: Sage.

Waters, Mary. 1999. *Black Identities: West Indian Immigrant Dreams and American Realities.* Cambridge MA: Harvard University Press.

———. 2001. "Growing Up West Indian and African American: Gender and Class Differences in the Second Generation." In *Island in the City: West Indian Migration to New York*, edited by Nancy Foner, 193–215. Los Angeles: University of California Press, Ltd.

Watkins-Owens, Irma. 2001. "Early Twentieth-Century Caribbean Women: Migration and Social Networks in New York City." In *Island in the City: West Indian Migration to New York*, edited by Nancy Foner, 25–51. Los Angeles: University of California Press, Ltd.

Wegenstein, Bernadette. 2012. *The Cosmetic Gaze: Body Modification and the Construction of Beauty*. Cambridge MA: MIT Press.

Weiss, Robert. 1994. *Learning from Strangers*. New York: Free Press.

Wilcot, Swithin. 1995. "'Women of Abandoned Character': Women and Protest in Jamaica, 1838–65." In *Engendering History: Caribbean Women in Historical Perspective*, edited by Verene Sheperd, Bridget Brereton, and Barbara Bailey, 279–95. New York: St. Martin's Press.

Wilk, Richard. 1993. "Miss World Belize: Globalism, Localism, and the Political Economy of Beauty." Paper presented at the Decennial Meeting of the Association of Social Anthropologists of the Commonwealth, Oxford, July.

Willis, Deborah, and Carla Williams. 2002. *The Black Female Body: A Photographic History*. Philadelphia: Temple University Press.

Wilson, Peter. 1995. *Crab Antics: A Caribbean Study of the Conflict between Reputation and Respectability*. Long Grove IL: Waveland Press.

Wood, Helen, and Beverley Skeggs. 2004. "Notes on Ethical Scenarios of Self on British Reality TV." *Feminist Media Studies* 4 (2): 205–8.

Zinn, Dorothy. 2005. "The Senegalese Immigrants in Bari: What Happens When the Africans Peer Back." In *Migration and Identity*, edited by Rina Benmayor and Andor Skotnes, 53–68. New Brunswick NJ: Transaction Publishers.

INDEX

Du Bois, Christine, 34–35; *Images of West Indians in the Mass Media*, 52

Du Bois, Kerwin: *Soca*, 89–90; "Too Real," 89–90

Du Bois, W. E. B., 111

economic mobility, 21–24, 27, 66–67, 103–6, 156–57, 160

economic neoliberalism, 160, 170–71

economic privilege, 14, 57

Edmondson, Belinda, 7, 18

education, 50, 54–55, 132–33

"embodied crisis" actions, 27, 113

embodied cultural citizenship: body image and, 118–19; identity and, 44, 76, 114–15; media and, 146, 148, 150–52, 169; negotiating and creating, 36–37, 155–56, 162; physical capital and, 26–27; respectability and performativity and, 123, 130, 156

embodied stratification, 159

entrepreneurship, 162–63

Ethiopian Jews, 53

ethnic niching, 48–49

ethnocentrism, 45–46, 48, 50, 53

Eurocentrism, 17, 26, 28, 90, 115

exoticization, 2, 71, 73, 169

Fanon, Franz, 141

fashion, 92, 102–4, 126–32, 152–53. *See also* dress

The Fat Black Woman's Poems (Nichols), 11–12

fatness, 11–14, 16, 22–23, 96, 168

femininity, 12, 13–14, 15–16, 18

films, Caribbean peoples in, 52

flexible citizenship, 64–66

flexible identities, 65–67, 72–73, 74, 114, 126

Foner, Nancy, 34, 35

Freeman, Carla, 162

gender roles, 36, 69, 120

"habitual" actions, 27

hair, 83–84, 176n5

Hall, Maruice M., 43

Hall, Stuart, 140, 141, 142, 146

Hart-Celler Immigration Bill, 31

health-care services, 32, 48–49

Herndon, April Michelle, 22–23

hierarchy and bodily forms, 22–24

Hintzen, Percy, 51

Hobson, Janell, 9, 17, 91, 120, 166

homeland bond, 33–34

Hottentot Venus, 8–9, 119, 163–64, 166, 168–69, 175n2

hybrid identities, 63–67

hybridity, cultural, 34, 64, 74

hypersexuality, 8, 52

identity, 54–76; accents and, 57–59; and being spectacles, 73–75; citizenship and nationhood and, 64–65; conceptions of Caribbean, 67–72; flexible, 65–67, 72–73, 74, 114, 126; media and, 141–42, 172; overview of, 34, 35, 41, 43, 45, 75–76; performativity and, 119, 176n1; racial, 78–80, 115

Images of West Indians in the Mass Media (Du Bois), 52

immigrants, Caribbean, 33–36, 45, 51, 56–57, 106

immigrants, first-generation: accents and, 57–59; as permanent foreigners, 54–57, 59–63, 114; respectability and, 121–26, 132–35; as study participants, 38

immigrants, second-generation: conceptions of Caribbean, 67–72; disruption of beauty ideals by, 116, 126–27, 136–37; dress and, 126–32; identity and, 63–68; scholarship on, 35; as spectacles, 73–75; as study participants, 38

immigrant women, role of, 36, 44–45

immigration, 30–33, 45–50, 176n4

inequality, 9–10, 46, 159–60

invisibility, 73–75

Jamaica: about, 3–5, 47; Caribbean media's focus on, 170, 171–72; emigration from, 32; respectability and, 122; U.S. immigrant views of, 69

"Jamaican-ization" of the Caribbean, 170

Justus, Joyce Bennett, 34

kalokagatheia, 110, 124–25, 128, 137–38

Kardashian, Kim, 165

Knowles, Beyoncé, 97, 108, 176n5

LaBennett, Oneka, 35, 36

Lavater, Johann Kaspar, 20

liminality, 63, 67–68

Lombroso, Cesare, 20–21

"Looking at Miss World" (Nichols), 11

Lopez, Jennifer: "Booty," 165

Lorde, Aude, 138

makeover television programs, 110–11, 147–48, 150–51

Makiesky-Barrow, Susan, 34

Mammy, 2–3, 163–64, 175n2

Mammy-Sapphire continuum, 2–3

marginalization: body size and, 1, 23, 156–58; clothing and, 104–6; color blindness and, 10, 46–47, 167–68; and embracement of thick body image, 114, 119, 160, 166–67; identity and, 62, 63, 66; media and, 108–10, 150; overview of, 45–48, 155

masculinization of black women, 9, 11

Mason, Katherine, 159–60

maturity and ideal body, 134–35

McCarran-Walter Act, 31

media, American: butt revolution and, 165; concentrated ownership of, 171; depiction of black women in, 51–52, 63, 107–8, 145–46, 164–65; engagement of, 139–43, 146–52, 177n4; opposition to body image in, 142–46; thin ideal and, 29, 108–12, 157; voluptuous ideal and, 94–96

media, Caribbean, 87–88, 152–53, 169–74

men, Caribbean, 101–2

men, Senegalese, 53

migration from the Caribbean, 30–33, 44–45, 176n4

Miller, Toby, 25

mimicry, 120–21, 126, 129–31, 146, 149, 156

Minaj, Nicki, 95; "Anaconda," 165